MOGUL MOM

ETSY SUCCESS

HOW TO MAKE A FULLTIME INCOME SELLING JEWELRY CRAFTS AND OTHER HANDMADE PRODUCTS ONLINE

KATHLEEN DONOVAN

Etsy Success - How to Make a Fulltime Income Selling Jewelry, Crafts, and Other Handmade Products Online

by Kathleen Donovan

Suite 264
2 Toronto St.
Toronto, ON Canada
M5C 2B5

For more information on this series,
please visit us on the web at

MogulMomBooks.com

TABLE OF CONTENTS

INTRODUCTION

Do You Dream of Making and Selling Jewelry Online?

Many people assume that a poor economy automatically translates into a reduction in jewelry purchases. While this may be true for high-priced costume jewelry, both men and women still want to adorn themselves with necklaces, bracelets, rings, and other jewelry items. Today, individuals of all ages are becoming increasingly suspicious of costume jewelry that is filled with lead and other dangerous metals.

Since many people are looking for relatively inexpensive jewelry options, they are turning to homemade jewelry fashioned by people that sell their creations online. For example, millions of people all over the world visit Etsy.com in order to look for fashionable homemade jewelry. Whether they're searching for items made with natural stones, glass beads, shells or other objects, shoppers are also willing to pay a reasonable price for jewelry that captures their attention.

If you have always wanted to make and sell jewelry, you can get started on making that dream come true immediately! Even if you only start by putting one or two pieces up for sale on Etsy.com, you are sure to be pleased when they sell. In fact, once you start selling your jewelry, you will be able to look at the world in a very different way. Instead of being like millions of other people trapped in dead-end jobs that are about to be lost, you will join thousands of other people that make a living right at home. When the world is filled with potential customers, you will never have to worry about where the next dollar will come from.

It is important to realize that unbridled warfare, governmental collapse, and many other problems are going to continue having a negative impact on the economy. Emotionally speaking, people are constantly looking for objects that have a personal feel. This is just one of the many reasons why handmade jewelry is becoming so popular. When individuals feel upset and distressed about things going on in their life, a piece of costume jewelry does not have the "human touch" that comes with handmade items. As someone that fashions homemade jewelry, you will be satisfying a very deep-seated need that cannot be filled any other way.

Today, thousands of people are making more money, and enjoying more freedom than they ever did when they were working at conventional jobs. Wouldn't you love to be able to fashion beautiful jewelry while sitting on a tropical beach? How would you feel if you could create beautiful homemade rings and bracelets while the snow flies around a luxury cabin in the mountains? If you simply dare to embrace your wildest dreams, you can make all of them come true.

A Brief History of Etsy

Even though Etsy.com was only founded in 2005, it has enjoyed a reasonable amount of success. The company was initially founded by Haim Schoppik, Chris Maguire and Robert Kalin. Within less than two years, Etsy.com garnered close to $2 million in sales. This has also translated into a boon for those who are interested in selling homemade and vintage wares. In fact, ever since May 2009, Etsy.com has been generating $10 million to $13 million in sales per month.

On average, for each seller, there are at least five buyer accounts. Therefore, anyone that is interested in selling on Etsy.com has an ideal opportunity to develop a steady stream of loyal customers from around the world. As an added bonus, the Web-based interface for Etsy is constantly being upgraded in order to provide better tools and more appealing storefronts.

MAKING A CAREER WITH CUSTOM JEWELRY IN THE MODERN WORLD

If you are interested in selling custom jewelry, you will need to do some planning to make sure that your designs are appealing and profitable. To begin, you should start thinking about a basic theme for your designs. This theme may focus around a particular emotion, an attempt to capture a period in history, or the symbolization of some culture. You may even want to use holidays, historical events, or newsworthy items for inspiration. Chances are, if you browse the Etsy.com Web site, you will get plenty of ideas about what other people are doing, as well as which designs and themes tend to be the most popular.

Once you select a theme, it will be time to start thinking about the materials you will use to craft each item. For example, if you decide to work with Celtic designs, you don't necessarily have to stay with stones and knots. Instead, you may decide to use seashells and other items in a way that blends the mystery of the sea with symbols that are reminiscent of this particular culture. While you are developing your signature pieces, you will need to take note of the cost for bulk quantities of each component. It is also very important to determine how long it will take you to fashion each piece of jewelry.

Without a question, if you are going to succeed as a custom jewelry designer, you will need to ensure that you make a profit. At the same time, you will always have to find that delicate balance between the cost of doing business, and the amount of money that consumers will pay for your products. Fortunately, Etsy.com is an ideal place for you to test individual products before you commit to purchasing a large inventory of jewelry components. No matter whether you put one piece up for sale, or an entire related collection, you will be able to find out fairly quickly if you should start developing other designs.

As a general rule of thumb, individuals that are successful in business know how to plan each aspect of their new venture in order to ensure that each component of the business enhances productivity and customer satisfaction. While you may initially feel tempted to focus on designing jewelry, you will also need to tend to other details related to your online image, as well as your store policies. At the very least, in the early stages of developing your business, you should spend an equal amount of time on developing this aspect of your business as you do on the actual production of jewelry items.

THE ADVANTAGES OF USING ETSY TO SELL YOUR HOMEMADE JEWELRY

There is no question that starting your own business can be filled with a number of challenges. That said, when you make your start with Etsy.com, you will enjoy at least three advantages. In fact, many people that get their start on Etsy.com stay there for years on end because they truly don't need to go anywhere else in order to make a reasonable amount of money.

LOW ADVERTISING FEES

In order to advertise an item on Etsy.com, you will only have to pay $.20 for the initial listing. Once the item sells, the site gains an additional 3.5 percent. This is much lower than what you would pay on any other Web site. At the same time, you will also gain access to millions of customers that already visit this site on a daily basis as they search for custom jewelry.

LARGE & ACTIVE CUSTOMER BASE

Even though eBay has a reputation for being one of the most popular online merchant sites, it has lost a significant amount of popularity in the last two years. In fact, a number of merchants that got fed up with certain policy changes at eBay actually decided to start selling their items at Etsy.com. Invariably, when these merchants moved, they also brought a sizable crowd of reliable customers along with them.

Today, many people prefer Etsy.com over other shopping sites because they are looking for good quality items at a low price. As the economy continues to get worse, you can rest assured that an increasingly number of people will find Etsy.com more appealing. This, in turn, means that items you advertise on this site will get even more exposure.

POWERFUL TOOLS AND DYNAMIC INTERFACE

Aside from having a loyal customer base, a merchant site must also be able to reach out to new people. Fortunately, the Etsy.com site features plenty of search engine-friendly components. This includes specialized tag features that help individual products gain a better ranking. You are also sure to enjoy taking advantage of site features that enable you to integrate your store with social networking sites, as well as many other venues.

CHAPTER ONE

Are You Ready?

BELIEVING IN YOUR TALENT

Even though your friends and family may offer positive comments about your creations, there may always be a nagging doubt in the back of your mind. Are they just trying to be nice? Will others like your creations so much that they will pay you a decent price? Invariably, believing in your talent may be difficult as you begin the process of selling homemade jewelry online.

Before you begin to market your products, it is extremely important to have faith in the fact that you have a special gift for creating worthwhile and meaningful jewelry. Chances are, you already realize that beauty is a matter of personal taste. Under these circumstances, you might want to set yourself a slightly different goal when it comes to evaluating your particular talent. At the very least, if others tell you that your designs are "beautiful," you can ask them what they feel about each piece.

Consider a situation where you are interested in selling jewelry that focuses on using glass beads. If you look online, you will see millions of necklaces made from the same materials. Nevertheless, as you browse through these listings, you are sure to find that at least one appeals to you more than the others. Can you define what that "extra something" is that sets one piece of jewelry apart from the others?

Interestingly enough, that special "something" has to do with your empathic sense of the piece. When a piece of jewelry stimulates your emotions in a positive way, or it fulfills some emotional sense, then it may not even matter what the piece looks like. Therefore, if you have doubts about your talent as a jewelry designer, you will need to look at each piece, and ask if it has an emotional resonance with a large audience of people. Without a question, if people are willing to talk about your jewelry and tie it to a feeling, or a sense of well-being, then you can safely assume that you have a special and recognizable talent.

GETTING READY TO DO BUSINESS

As an artist, you will have to shift your mental gears many times in order to take care of routine business needs. This includes keeping accurate accounting records, advertising, taking care of your customers, and making sure that you have all the supplies required to create each piece of jewelry. No matter how much you may be tempted to place a low emphasis in these matters, it will only hurt your business in the end. If you would rather spend the majority of your time working on creating jewelry, you would be well served by delegating tasks that you have no interest in. At the very least, this will ensure that the work gets done in a way that does not sacrifice the overall stability of the company.

Today, there are very few companies that have enough money to meet payroll. Under these circumstances, you may need to make use of other options to help meet the basic administrative needs of your company. This may include asking family members to help out. On the other hand, if you are looking for professional and qualified assistance, you can always make use of outsourcing venues to hire a virtual administrator. This will enable you to contract for the services of people all over the world in an affordable way.

MANAGING YOUR SCHEDULE AND MEETING DEADLINES

When you first start out in your new business, you will most likely spend an enormous amount of time filling orders. During the process of deciding how much to charge, you should know exactly how much time it makes to recreate each of you signature pieces. If you add an extra 10 or 15 minutes on to that, you can figure out the approximate cost of labor. This, in turn, will be of immense benefit if you find that you are swamped with orders and need to hire someone to help you do the work.

In a sense, when you own your own business, there is no such thing as working "9 to 5" – and then simply forgetting that the business exists. No matter whether you spend time checking your business emails, meeting tax filing obligations, or simply trying to finish up a rush order, there are always times when your schedule will have to be reprioritized. That said, there are still some measures that you can use to keep some semblance of normality to your life.

To begin with, it is very important to schedule buffer days, or at least hours, into your schedule. Rather that simply assume you can take the weekends off, you will be better served by blocking one free day into your schedule for every three days that you work. While this will invariably mean working on the weekends, at least you will be able to meet your business needs and still have some time to yourself.

If you are trying to meet a deadline, there is nothing worse than trying to do so without a time buffer. No matter how you look at it, supplies may come in late, equipment can fail, and your family may get sick. Unfortunately, many business owners find that "Murphy's Law" can go into full and extensive force at all the wrong moments. This is just one of many reasons why setting deadlines with care is so important. As a general rule of thumb, you should not take an order if you cannot manage to build in an extra day's buffer and still meet the deadline.

CUSTOMER SUPPORT

No matter how you look at it, the success of your business depends on happy customers. Inevitably, the level of satisfaction will include a number of factors; the quality of the workmanship, timeliness of delivery, and price. If you are going to interact personally with each customer, your ability to create a polite and comfortable environment is also critical.

If you think about yourself as a customer, then you should be able to determine what you need to do in order to serve the needs of your customers. Consider a situation in which you want to buy a shell necklace that you found at an online store. What kinds of things are you thinking about as you look at that piece of jewelry? Even though it may appeal to you, any number of questions may be going through your head.

Let's say that you decide to buy the necklace, and that the designer lives all the way on the other side of the country. Depending on the price, you may well be wondering if you will be paying for something that you will never receive. In these troubling times, that can be a huge concern for a customer. Under these circumstances, you will most likely want to look and see if the merchant has a good reputation with other buyers. As a merchant, if you do not ship items on time, or forget to send them out, then you will not have happy customers or a good reputation.

Regardless of whether or not a merchant has a good standing, there may still be customers that are willing to spend money on a product if it catches their eye. While this gives marginal merchants a chance to improve their standing, there is still another pitfall.

As you may be aware, certain types of jewelry may be very fragile. Without a question, customer service in these situations is going to involve packaging each item in order to prevent breakage. You will also need to set prices high enough to cover shipping insurance. Even if only one out of 100 items arrive broken, at least you will not lose your investment in the product.

As a customer support specialist, you will be dealing with complete strangers on a daily basis. They will write to you via email, pop up on your messenger, and attempt to make contact all hours of the day and night. It is very important to make sure that you are comfortable with these elements of customer support. If you cannot send a polite email to someone, then you will need to make sure that you are capable of taking a step back from the situation until you can do so. No matter what the situation is, you will need to conduct yourself in a professional and firm manner.

In a sense, when it comes to customer support, you need to be every bit as confident in your ability to work with people as you are in your skills as a jewelry designer. If you do not feel that you are good with people, then you might want to take a course on how to go about managing these interactions. Today, there are plenty of online courses, e-books, and guides that will teach you how to communicate via email, as well as in chat. That said, if you are certain that you don't want to handle this part of the business, you can hire a virtual administrator instead.

PROJECT AND PRODUCT MANAGEMENT – THE PRODUCTION SIDE

There is an enormous difference between creating a signature piece of jewelry and replicating it. Among other things, when you are in the process of creating a new design, you will spend an enormous amount of time thinking about the shape of the piece, as well as individual components. During this process, time will most likely be one of the least important factors. On the other hand, when it comes to replicating the design, you will need to think about your profit margin and quality.

If you want to create a bracelet that features 30 glass beads, for example, then you will need to make sure that you have enough of each item on hand. During the process of creating the signature piece, you may simply look through what you have in order to assemble the bracelet. Unfortunately, if you don't know where you bought each component, you may have a very hard time coping with orders that come in.

As a jewelry designer, you may wind up having hundreds of different components in your working inventory. Many people that start a home jewelry business make the mistake of organizing these components based on how quickly they can reach for a particular item during the replication process. While you can still create that type of system, you should also make sure that each tray or bin includes very clear information about the origin of each component. For example, rather than rely on SKU numbers, you should also make it a point to add the name of the company, as well as a short description of the item.

During the process of creating signature pieces, you should also place similar tags on each component. While you may find it tedious to label every single bead or other item, at least you will not be wasting time trying to match this information up on a paper map. As an added bonus, when you place the information right on the jewelry piece, you can also add an additional tag that will serve as a summary.

When it comes to producing jewelry, you will often find that it is cheaper to buy individual components in bulk. Ideally, you should be able to have enough components on hand to meet daily needs without running out. Rather than simply relying on one company, you should always keep a list of suppliers for each item. At the very least, if one company is back-ordering your supplies, then you can look to the next one on your list. You can use databases and spreadsheets to help you keep your primary suppliers list organized, as well as your secondary and tertiary sources.

FEAR OF FAILURE – AND SUCCESS

There is no question that pop psychology has created an enormous belief in the "fear of success." Rather than get trapped in that ideology, you can, and should, prepare yourself for success. For example, if you believe in the "fear of success," then you may be afraid to think, dream and plan for massive orders. In fact, you may decide that you are afraid of being swamped with work. As with anything else in the business environment, preparing for success will eventually lead to success.

In this situation, all you really need to do is make sure that you know how long it takes to make each piece of jewelry. If you wind up with a certain number of orders, make sure that you have enough people on hand to help you meet your obligations. No matter whether you keep a short list of family members or people in your neighborhood, you can, and should be able to get those orders filled. Once you find that you have a steady number of large orders coming in, taking the next step to hire full-time employees will become an easy and manageable goal.

Ironically, when it comes to success, your biggest problems may have nothing to do with being prepared to manufacture and ship your products. Rather, you may find that tax burdens can drive you into bankruptcy. Unfortunately, researchers have not come up with a way to assess the impact of taxes when it comes to business failure. On the other hand, it should be noted that the vast majority of new businesses fail within two years. Many of these businesses take out loans or use credit cards to meet production needs, only to find out that they must still pay taxes on their "profit."

Aside from sales tax, you should make sure that your prices include an 80 percent extra markup on top of your profit just for taxes. This will include payroll tax, value-added taxes, healthcare tax, licensing taxes, income tax, inventory tax, equipment/asset tax, and corporate shareholder tax, as well as complimentary taxes at the state and local levels. While you may not like the reality of an 80 percent markup for taxes, you will invariably find that failing to do so will leave a gaping hole in your budget. Without a question, you should always keep this in mind when it comes time to vote. In fact, you should always seek to educate friends, family members and customers about the cost of taxes and their impact on your product cost.

When it comes to the fear of failure, there is no such thing as a philosophical outlook. As with the "fear of success," you will need to be prepared for problems. In most cases, you will be wise to come up with a list of problems that may occur with each product that you design. When you go through this list, you should come up with at least three methods for dealing with the problem, as well as the names of three people that will help you manage the situation. This will preserve your ability to meet customer needs, deal with problems as they come up, and enable you to keep your focus on moving forward.

If you want to know whether or not you have overcome your fears, there is nothing like putting your first item up for sale. At the very least, if you do not feel confident, you can limit the number of orders that you will accept in a given time period. Typically, as you grow more confident with advertising, production and sales, you will be able to increase the number of orders that you feel comfortable handling.

PREPARING TO DEAL WITH FEEDBACK ON YOUR CREATIONS

Even though a customer may be every excited about a particular piece of jewelry, they may feel differently once they receive it. Without a question, if the item is broken, or not packaged properly, your customer may be very upset. This is just one of many reasons why you should always have a care plan in place to manage these issues. While shipping insurance will eventually help you recapture the cost of broken items, you should still make sure that you can send a replacement to your customer as quickly as possible. Ideally, you should have at least one or two extra pieces on hand to mail out, as well as surplus components in your inventory that will be used just for that purpose.

Unfortunately, you will always come across customers that are not satisfied with the items that you offer for sale. Depending on the situation, you may want to offer a refund, or simply accept poor feedback. Regardless of the situation, you should not take these matters personally. Over time, if you conduct yourself in an appropriate way, you will still have plenty of satisfied customers that will tip the balance in your favor. That said, if you feel that the customer has some type of agenda, you can make an effort to comment on that feedback, as well as seek to have it removed via site administrators.

HOW TO KNOW YOU ARE READY TO PUT YOUR CREATIONS ONLINE

As a general rule of thumb, if you aren't sure that you are ready to offer your creations to the public, then you are not ready. While listening for this sense can be difficult, once you experience it, there will no longer be a question in your mind. Oddly enough, this sense may occur even if you have not taken all of the steps to prepare your business. Rather than simply ignore what you are feeling, you can still make limited offerings in order to get started.

In some cases, you may have taken all of the necessary steps to prepare your business. Nevertheless, you may still be wondering if the time is right. Under these circumstances, you may have to look a bit deeper to find out why you are still hesitating. For example, if you are currently receiving unemployment benefits or public assistance, you may be afraid that success will prevent you from making use of these services. Rather than continuing to be afraid, it is important to realize that these benefits will expire eventually. Therefore, you might just as well get started on building your business. Even though you may not know how it will turn out, at least you will be moving forward with your life. As may be expected, if you are truly afraid that you will wind up in a worse situation, you can make sure that friends or family members are available to help you out if needed.

No matter what you do in life, there always comes a moment when you will either move forward with your plans or never enjoy the chance to be successful. If you give it some thought, you will realize that you have already come through many similar points in your life. Among other things, when you were learning to drive, you most likely had to pass a road test. Nevertheless, the real test of whether or not you could drive actually came when you got into the car alone for the first time. When it comes to your new business, you will know you are ready on the day that you decide to open your store and move forward.

CHAPTER TWO

Defining Yourself and Your Customer

SOME REASONS WHY YOU CANNOT BE "ALL THINGS TO ALL PEOPLE"

In the early stages of running a business, there is always a tendency to worry about every penny of potential income. As a jewelry designer, you may be tempted to change your niche based on what seems popular. For example, if you prefer to design Egyptian jewelry, you might feel tempted to work with Celtic designs because they seem more popular.

It is very important to realize that jewelry fashion is every bit as changeable and unpredictable as clothing. Therefore, even though one type of jewelry may be popular today, it may not be popular tomorrow. While you may want to create one or two lead pieces to attract customers to your store, the main bulk of your inventory should still be an accurate reflection of your niche and personal interests.

As a general rule of thumb, holding to your niche enables you to ensure that you can deliver products in a timely manner. If you let go of this one simple element of your business, you will quickly find that you cannot produce enough jewelry to make a reasonable amount of money. You may even find that constantly trying to keep up with new "trends" will create a situation in which you cannot even meet the needs of the customers you are trying to attract.

Any business owner will tell you that the decision to keep or discontinue certain products can be very complicated. That said, there are a few things you can do to help assess when it is time to stick with a particular design, and when it is time to change. This may include looking to see if you have large customer accounts dedicated to a specific design, as well as what the overall demand is for similar jewelry. While you cannot cater to every single person that comes across your store, you should still make an effort to satisfy as many as you can with the resources that you have available

CHOOSING YOUR NICHE AND STAYING WITH IT

There are many different ways to define a jewelry niche. This may include only offering necklaces, bracelets or other items. You may also want to identify your niche based on a particular design or series of components. Before you start creating signature pieces, it may be worth your effort to study trends in homemade jewelry. While there is no way to predict what will be popular from one day to the next, you should still start off by isolating current trends.

When it comes to identifying your niche, you should never overlook an opportunity to define the niche. Invariably, it is your personal creativity and the overall appeal of your message that will determine your success in business. Consider a situation where you have decided that you want to sell enameled bracelets. As you look for similar products, you may note that the most popular designs have flowers on them. Ideally, the bulk of your signature pieces should make use of flowers. Regardless of whether you create some with large, exotic flowers, or small and dainty ones, your jewelry will still appeal to a large number of people.

It is very important to realize that people are not going to be interested in enameled bracelets with flowers on them forever. While they may still enjoy this type of bracelet, they may also want different designs. Under these circumstances, you can start looking for news trends and other information that will help you shape the market to your liking. For example, if you notice a number of news stories about a particular type of animal, you may want to dedicate one or two bracelets to that animal. Even though these particular bracelets may not initially be big sellers, your customers will not forget about them. At some point, when they are looking for something different, they may just decide that an animal bracelet will be more appealing than a flower one.

BRANDING YOUR PRODUCT LINE

Even though your jewelry may have a specific design, you will need a logo to help define your business. Consider that the most famous companies in the world are known by their logo. Even if the mascot or company name has nothing to do with the product, people will still hone in on the logo when it comes to buying different products. For example, if you like Pepsi ™ cola, then you may react more favorably to sodas produced by the same manufacturer. In fact, if you are browsing in your local store, the Pepsi ™ logo may catch your eye and alert you to the new product.

Without a question, if you want to establish repeat trade with consumers, you will need a memorable and appealing logo. It will also be of some help to make sure that you use a color scheme that fits with your message and designs. Unfortunately, many people today stick with trite and stereotyped images and colors for branding purposes. For example, if you are going to create Celtic jewelry, you may automatically think that you need to use green and silver in your logo. On the other hand, if you want a contemporary look, there is nothing wrong with a logo that includes red or blue in it. While you logo may look different from what others would expect, at least it will stand out.

Oddly enough, few people think about font that will be used as part of the logo. That said, even though you may have a memorable mascot, the letters used in the name of your business are also very important. Consider that the lettering for Pepsi ™ and Coca-Cola ™ are a very important part of the product image. Interestingly enough, if you look at published trademarks, you will find that a good number of them use special fonts for the text.

FINDING YOUR CUSTOMERS

Typically, when you open a store on Etsy.com, there will already be plenty of people looking for items to buy. On the other hand, it is also very important to look for ways to draw other people to your store. This may include working with email campaigns, joining relevant groups, and making use of social networking to advertise your products. You may also want to think about finding ways to target specific geographic regions. This will be of immense benefit if you are going to create jewelry for specific holidays, or items dedicated to a specific event.

When you are seeking to define your customer base, it is important to think about other interests they might have. This can be of immense benefit if you want to start a new jewelry trend, and then continue to stay at the front of the market. For example, if you want to shift attention toward designs that include animals on them, you can visit groups dedicated to animal issues. Regardless of whether you join groups on Facebook.com, Myspace.com, Yahoo.com, or Ning.com, individuals in those groups will provide you with plenty of inspiration, as well as an excellent view of their attitudes and ideas. If you can capture that in your jewelry, you have an excellent chance of capturing current popular trends.

GETTING TO KNOW YOUR CUSTOMERS

No matter how you look at it, maintaining a professional image can be difficult while you are trying to learn more about your potential audience. In a similar way, when someone buys a piece of jewelry from you, it is very important to make sure that you maintain an empathic sense of him or her. While you may not want to communicate with each person on a daily basis, you should still make some effort to stay in regular contact. At the very least, if you create a particular piece of relevant jewelry down the road, you can always invite them to have a look at it.

Today, many online business owners make use of newsletters and other tools to help gain feedback from established customers. If you offer news about jewelry trends, this is an ideal time to simply ask each person to let you know what they think of the information you provided. Aside from keeping your business name relevant, you may also gain some important information about which trends will die out fastest. This, in turn, can help you modulate your inventory and shape future signature pieces.

When it comes to learning more about your customers, you should never overlook the basics of making a purchase. Do you hate walking into a store with messy aisles and grouchy clerks? Chances are, your customers feel the same way. During the process of getting to know your customers, consider how they will view your online store. At the very least, you can offer a survey to find out if they think your store is too confusing, among other questions about the actual product.

CHAPTER THREE

Setting Up Your Store

DOES YOUR STORE NAME MATTER?

Many entrepreneurs struggle to name their business. In many cases, they wind up using some part of their name and a description of the product. For example, if person's name is Macie Smith, they may name their store "Macie's Celtic Jewelry." Unfortunately, that naming method will not stand out when compared to "Joan's Home Celtic Jewelry," "Sadie's Fashions," and so on. On the other hand, if the name of your store is too bizarre, people will still have a hard time remembering it.

As you may be aware, many people do not buy an item the first time that they see it. In fact, they may come back to your listing two or three times before they make a final decision. This is just one of many reasons why it is very important to have an appealing and distinctive store name. If you are going to sell jewelry at Etsy.com, you should at least look at the names of stores dedicated to selling jewelry. While you are looking through these names, try to identify the most common threads. From there, you can ask yourself which names and ideas are missing.

Even though it may take some time, you should never use a store name that will simply look like everyone else's. Aside from making it harder to define your business, using names that are too similar to others may create legal problems. These could include issues related to trademark and patent violations. If you think that a name is too close to something else that already exists, the best thing you can do is try to come up with something different.

THREE PATHS TO A GREAT LOGO

While you may not have any problems coming up with fantastic jewelry designs, you may find it a bit harder to create a logo that will enhance your business image. But coming up with an incredible looking logo may not be as hard as you initially thought. Even if you cannot draw the image, or come up with tangible ideas, there are still ways to ensure that your logo is appealing and creditable.

LOOK AT EXISTING TRADEMARKS

If you are going to conduct business in the United States, you can look through an online catalog of all registered trademarks in the United States (www. uspto.gov/index.jsp). Even though you cannot use any of these designs for your own business, they will still give you plenty to think about. Chances are, you will be amazed at how many symbols are used on a daily basis to define businesses that you never even knew existed. As may be expected, if you live in a country other than the United States, you can still use this Web site for ideas. You may also want to see if the trademark office in your own country offers a similar resource.

DRAW SOMETHING IN YOUR ENVIRONMENT

There is no question that your household is filled with hundreds of ordinary items. On the other hand, if you look with the eye of an artist, you may see an interesting shape, or pattern that can be turned into a logo. For example, if you look on your desk, you may be interested in the arraignment of pens, pencils and highlighters. If you convert those to feather quills, or something else relevant to jewelry design, you may be able to come up with a unique logo.

HIRE A PROFESSIONAL LOGO DESIGNER

In some cases, you may know exactly what kind of logo you want to create. Unfortunately, if you have problems drawing stick people, then you may have a hard time creating something more complicated. Rather than using clip art, you can hire a professional logo designer. These individuals can easily take a written description of what you want and turn it into an appealing image. As an added bonus, many logo designers can also make recommendations about color schemes, fonts and other elements of the logo.

CREATING AN EYE-POPPING AVATAR

Many people are tempted to simply use a picture of themselves, their product or their logo when it comes to an avatar for forums and stores. While you should strive to create a consistent image, your avatar should not look like you simply used the first thing that came along. At the very least, if you are going to use your logo, you should spice it up, or try to make it look a bit different. This may include using image editing filters to create different effects, as well as overlying a piece of signature jewelry on top of the logo.

As with so many other things, creating an eye-popping avatar depends on context and timing. If everyone around you is using windswept versions of their logo for an avatar, yours will wind up looking like a copy. At the very least, look at original avatars, then see if you can create something different. That said, if you want to fit into the group, then you can always create an avatar that fits the stereotype for your niche.

THREE PATHS TO AN ENGAGING BIOGRAPHY: DEFINING YOURSELF AS A UNIQUE CHARACTER

As you browse through the merchant stores at Etsy.com, you will find dozens of profiles. In each case, the author is trying to convey information about him/herself that will form a link to the reader. Ideally, the bio should help readers make up their mind about buying a particular piece of jewelry. As you fashion your own bio, it is very important to think about what makes you a unique and special person. If you cannot define yourself as an individual and as an artist, you may have a harder time selling your jewelry.

When creating your bio, you may want to talk about art styles that interest you, or why you decided to start crafting jewelry. Some people also talk about hobbies and personal interests. While you may not feel comfortable discussing politics or religion, it may still be of some help to define an interest in common causes. That said, you may also decide to create a bio that has a light and comical feel to it. Without a question, if you can make someone laugh or smile for just a few seconds, that may be just enough to get them to buy something from you.

THINK ABOUT WHAT DRAWS YOU TO OTHER PEOPLE

As a businessperson, you will always need to think about things from the customer's perspective. Even though everyone is unique and special, your opinions usually aren't so different from those of the vast majority of people around you. Would you buy a piece of jewelry from someone that uses words or phrases that you can't understand? What about a person that indicates they don't care how many other pieces of jewelry out there look just like the ones you are about to buy?

When you first meet someone, you usually have a sense about whether or not you will like them. Invariably, people will tell you not to judge others based on these first impressions. That said, when someone reads your bio, that first impression is all they have to go on. Make that introduction as appealing as possible. While saying "Hello" may seem trite, you should not overlook common politeness. In fact, offering some type of greeting will serve to capture your reader's attention, and help them to focus on what you are saying.

During the process of creating your bio, you should make an effort to pick out 10 that have the most appeal to you, as well as 10 from the top merchants on the site where you want to do business. As you study these bios, look for common threads, as well as things that make each bio different. From there, you should be able to look at your own life and jewelry, and come up with an appealing and realistic bio.

HIRE A PROFESSIONAL WRITER

As with visual designs, there are also individuals that excel when it comes to putting words on paper. If you are not one of those people, you may wind up frustrated when you can't seem to find the right words, or convey a particular sentiment. Fortunately, there are many freelance writers online that can help you. Once you tell them a little bit about yourself, they can easily take your information and turn it into a convincing and appealing bio.

THE IMPORTANCE OF HIGH-QUALITY PHOTOS

When you share pictures of your jewelry among friends and family members, they will look at the images with an understanding of who you are as a person. They will also take the extra time to see past poor focus, poor lighting, and other details that prevent them from gaining a good sense of the jewelry in the image. On the other hand, when someone is browsing through Etsy.com, or some other Web site, they will take less than a second to look at your offerings before moving on to the next store. Therefore, even if your jewelry truly is the best on the marketplace, poor quality pictures will never help you prove your point.

High quality photos are also invaluable when it comes to creating different sized images. For example, you may feel very tempted to simply create low-resolution images that will look good as thumbnails. If someone clicks on those images, however, the larger versions may appear grainy and distorted. Only post high-resolution photos, and be sure to convey as much information about the jewelry as possible.

HOW TO GET THE BEST PHOTOS

Unfortunately, when it comes to photographing jewelry, you will need to go through a process of trial and error. Items that are made from glass beads will usually have different reflection characteristics than ones made from metal. You may find that it will be easier to photograph some items outdoors, while others will look better on a white background.

As you may be aware, quality photos may not come from cheap cameras. If you do not have a good quality camera, it may be worth your while to take the items in question to a professional photographer. In fact, you may even be able to ask photographers based in a local department store if they will take pictures of your jewelry. If you bring along just one or two pieces at a time, they may be willing to help you.

Individuals that are determined to take their own pictures may want to try renting a camera, or borrowing one from a friend or family member. Unless you are going to create dozens of new signature pieces every single day, it may not make much sense to buy an expensive camera. On the other hand, once your business is established, you may decide that you have a need for it. At that stage, a used camera may be more suitably priced. Since high quality cameras tend to be more complicated to work with, you will be well served by taking courses that will teach you how to use them to the greatest advantage.

Once you are satisfied with the clarity of each photo, you may still need to do some work to make the images as appealing as possible. Make sure the item is centered in the photo, and remove any background. The last thing you will want to do is have a piece of jewelry that is overshadowed by garish colors or anything else that will distract attention from what you are trying to sell. Today, most people use methods to create a white background for each item.

When you are trying to enhance a picture of a person, you will most likely want to create an oval frame, or some other design. Unfortunately, when you are trying to sell jewelry, making these kinds of frames will just add a level of distraction that will prevent potential buyers from focusing on the details of the actual item. At the same time, when you use these kinds of backgrounds, the color schemes that you find appealing may actually be offensive to potential buyers. In most cases, you cannot go wrong with a simple white or black background.

HOW TO WRITE ITEM DESCRIPTIONS

As a general rule of thumb, descriptions should start off with clear and concise details about the item. You may want to name some of the elements used, as well as any special features. This is also an ideal place to mention if other sizes, colors, or complementary pieces are available.

Depending on the amount of room available, you may want to write a little bit about the meaning of symbols used in the jewelry. You may also want to discuss the inspiration that went into the piece, as well as how you feel about it. Many people also like to use the product description to name suitable occasion for wearing a specific item.

When you want to describe your jewelry, it is important to draw a balance between describing each piece, and telling a story that attracts the reader. In a sense, the words you use to define the jewelry are every bit as important as the image. At the very least, when the reader goes back to look at the image they should see it in a new and meaningful context. This might include seeing themselves wearing the item to a special party, or seeing how delighted someone else will be to receive the jewelry as a gift. Regardless of the story that you choose to tell, your reader should always believe that buying the item will lead to some type of benefit.

MANAGING YOUR INVENTORY

If you walk into a department store, there is nothing worse than finding empty shelves. In a similar way, your customers will not be happy if their items are constantly put on back order. Ideally, you should have at least one or two replications of each piece of jewelry available for sale. Once you find that some items are more popular than others, you can devote more time to replicating them.

It is also very important to set aside at least one or two pieces from each design for the purposes of replacing items that are lost or broken during the shipping process. As aggravating as these situations can be, you should make every attempt to ensure that your customer's needs will be met as quickly as possible.

You may also want to keep track of items that break often, and think about replacing components that do not hold up well during the shipping process.

When it comes to managing inventory, you should always make sure that items are stored in a way that makes them easy to grab for shipping purpose. This includes putting labels on packages so that you do not have to guess what is inside. As may be expected, making sure that you have enough shipping supplies on hand is also a vital part of managing your inventory. Ideally, you should set aside at least one room for processing orders, and then use a separate room for the actual fabrication of each item.

ETSY INSIDER TIP

POSITIONING FOR LOW COST AND HIGH VOLUME

Logically speaking, in the current economy, expensive items will not sell as well as cheap ones. On the other side of the coin, you will need to sell more items in order to make a reasonable profit. Most people that succeed at Etsy.com try to keep their prices in the $5.00 to $40.00 range. While lower-end prices may make it harder to meet your tax burden, you can still try to offer some pieces at a lower price in order to draw customer attention.

If you are going to use the "low price – high volume" strategy, you will need to work very hard to keep your expenses low. In most cases, buying components in bulk will be your main opportunity to save some money. Unfortunately, if you are planning on not counting the cost of labor, then you are likely to find that you cannot afford to pay someone else, plus take care of your tax obligations. Under no circumstance should you take on business or personal debt if the "low price – high volume" strategy leads you into a bottleneck. You will be better served by raising your prices, or looking for some other way to manufacture the items at a cheaper price.

CHAPTER FOUR

Marketing On Etsy.com

TIMING YOUR LISTINGS

hances are, when it comes to doing a series of things, you tend to get them done faster when you complete them in batches. Unfortunately, if you have 10 different items to put up for sale on Etsy. com, posting them all at once will not be of much good. Since the Web site features all new items on its homepage, you will only get one chance to draw the attention of random people visiting the site. On the other hand, if you create a new post every few minutes, then you will have a much better chance of attracting the attention of more people.

Most people choose to create their listings every two or three hours. You should also consider the time of day when your target audience is most likely online and looking for jewelry. For example, if you are targeting customers in the Northeastern United States, then the peak number of visitors will show up between 5 p.m. and 8 p.m. EST. You may also want to post more products during that time period in order to keep at least one of your ads showing on the Etsy.com homepage.

When it comes to timing your Etsy.com jewelry postings, you should also consider the day of the week. As you may be aware, people tend to be more inclined to spend money when they have just gotten paid. While you may want to put some teasers out earlier in the week, targeting Thursdays through the weekend will usually garner more sales.

Depending on the type of jewelry that you are selling, the time of year may also be very important. For example, if you created a series of pieces for a specific holiday, you will be well served by posting during the season when people are most likely shopping for those items. While you may want to leave one or two examples of holiday jewelry in your store, you may not notice many sales during the non-holiday season.

Interestingly enough, if you are looking for customers that want to give jewelry for a birthday, there are also ideal times of the year. In particular, you will find that more babies are born in November than any other month of the year. If you analyze statistics from specific countries, you may be able to uncover other trends that will help you select optimal posting days.

There is no question that you should always make an effort to have items on Etsy.com's homepage in order to attract the attention of random browsers. On the other hand, if you are interesting in generating as many sales as possible in a short period of time, you will still need to saturate the homepage during peak hours and calendar dates. Once you grow accustomed to identifying when buyers are most likely to be online, you will also have a better chance of enhancing all your other marketing efforts.

MAKING USE OF THE ETSY MESSAGE BOARDS

The Etsy.com community message boards can be used to your advantage. Among other things, they give you an opportunity to interact with your potential customers in a very direct and personal way. While you are sharing information about jewelry, you are sure to attract the attention of people that resonate with you on a more personal level. This, in turn, can make it much easier to generate sales if they visit your store.

When you post comments on the Etsy.com message boards, you will also have a chance to leave a link to your store. No matter whether you put it in your signature line, or somewhere in the text of your comment, people will click on it for the sake of curiosity. That said, creating comments that encourage people to click on the link will also be of benefit.

It may take a little bit of extra effort to get people to click on your link. Unfortunately, link spammers and the fear of malicious malware sites make some people hesitant to visit sites they are not familiar with. On the bright side, once people start recognizing you as someone with whom they share a rapport, you will have a better chance of getting them to click on your links.

Chances are, when you are interested in a good book, you will turn the pages as fast as possible in order to find out what happens next. Likewise, when generating comments for the Etsy.com message board, you can use "to be continued" or "see this link to find out more" in order to get people to visit your store. While this may help increase the number of clicks, you will also have to deliver on your promise to satisfy the reader's curiosity.

When you are trying to market through message boards, you will need to get potential buyers to invest time. In some cases, if someone takes an interest in what you are writing, they may feel more inclined to buy once they visit your store. Ideally, your store-based sales pitch should be aligned with the comments you placed on the forum. While you may want to change your slant to accommodate a more traditional sales pitch, it is still important to make sure your audience realizes at an unconscious level that they have already invested the resource of time. Once potential buyers feel more familiar with you from this perspective, they will be more inclined to make a purchase from you, rather than someone else that they don't know as well.

USING SHOWCASE SPOTS

Showcase spots enable you to highlight some of your best work in a widely viewed location on a Web site. While you may not want to spend the money to create showcase spots for every single piece of jewelry that you have for sale, it may still be of benefit to put at least one or two items in the showcase. At the very least, if you created a new design, or notice that some items are very popular, a showcase spot will invariably boost visibility.

Showcase spots are also an ideal place to make use of sales pitches that will ensure viewers look at other items in your store. For example, if you created a set of earrings that feature cats, then you might want to place a few lines of text about a matching bracelet or necklace. In a similar way, if you create jewelry for men and women, then you can use showcase spots to direct attention to the appropriate items.

When using Etsy.com showcase spots, you should also find out what other merchants are placing in their showcases. Invariably, as viewers browse through showcase items, you will need to make sure that yours stand out. Unfortunately, if everyone else is using the word "look," then your advertisement will simply blend in to the crowd if you use the same exact word. That said, there is nothing to stop you from using "l@@k, or some other spelling variation to draw attention.

As you may be aware, descriptive titles are very important. While your description should not be too brief, cramming excessive details into the description will confuse your reader. That said, when it comes to your showcase items, you may want to include two or three extra words for the sake of grabbing attention. Typically, if you can get people to invest a few extra seconds in reading the title, then there is a better chance they will click on it to read more.

CREATING TREASURY LISTS

A number of merchants that sell items on Etsy. com actually have two separate accounts. One account is often used for the store, while the second one is used to create treasury lists. Typically, when someone sees one of your items on this type of list, they will also place a higher value on it.

Consider a situation in which a viewer is looking for Christmas jewelry. Even though you may use the word "Christmas" in the title for each advertisement, dozens of other merchants will do the same thing. Therefore, you will need to find some other way to capture the attention of viewers that saw your ad but did not pay much attention to it.

When viewers begin browsing treasury lists, they will not be thinking as much about the fact that a merchant is trying to make a sales pitch. Therefore, if you can spark some curiosity with a treasury list, viewers will be more inclined to visit your site. Among other things, you may want to use questions in the titles ("What does Grandma REALLY want for Christmas?"), or words that generate curiosity in your particular niche ("Junk in the Trunk; 100% Recycled Antique Jewelry")

HOLDING CONTESTS

Even though you will always be the primary designer for your store, it is still important to find out what shoppers are looking for in terms of jewelry designs. In some cases, you may be surprised to find that shoppers have ideas of their own about specific patterns and colors. While they may not contact you and ask for specific jewelry items, they may be more inclined to share their thoughts during a contest.

Because not everyone can win the main prize, some potential customers will feel unhappy when the winner is announced. Depending on the situation, this may actually detract from your store. Therefore, if you are going to run a contest, you should try to make sure that everyone gets something.

If you do not want to ship free jewelry or prizes all over the world to "contest winners," (READ: consolation prizes), consider offering free online wares. This might include a free game that viewers can play on their cell phone, premium content newsletters, or something else that they will interact with during their spare time. These freebies give you an opportunity to present additional sales pitches, as well as ensure that your store remains relevant to individual users.

DISCOUNTS AND PROMOTIONAL CODE OFFERS

Most people want to drive a car with a powerful engine. This, in turn, means that the engine must generate a satisfying roar as it speeds up. Some time ago, certain car manufacturers used this information to create vehicles that would emit more noise than usual at lower speeds. Therefore, a person that was accelerating would believe the car seemed more powerful than it actually was.

During the process of working with discounts, you may find it useful to think like a car dealer that wants to keep costs low, while selling for as high a price as possible. Under these circumstances, you can use higher "regular" prices in order to show a larger mark down. While this may help in a small store, it needs to be used with caution in larger stores.

Consider a situation where you are trying to sell 10 enamel bracelets with different images on them. If you create a 50 percent discount for one design, you may be inclined to make it look like you are charging a higher initial price for that bracelet. When viewers look at other bracelets in your store, they will realize that the initial price for them is much lower. At the very least, you should make sure that your pre-discount prices are consistent with other prices in your store.

When you are working with discounts and promo codes, you will need to draw a delicate balance that will protect your profit margin, as well as ensure that your customers think they are getting a good deal. Invariably, this balance will also depend on how much your competitors are charging for similar products.

In the long run, discounts will work in your favor if you do not use them on a regular basis. Unfortunately, if buyers know that you are going to drop your price in a week or two, they will simply wait for that event to occur. At the very least, if you are going to offer a discount, you should not let it create a reduction in demand.

Many people prefer to create discounts that are based on the purchase of other items in the store. For example, if you are having problems generating sales for one type of jewelry, you may want to offer discounts when the piece is purchased with something that is more popular. At the very least, if the individual winds up liking the discounted item, they may come back and buy other items in the series.

If you are looking for other ways to use promotional codes and discounts, you can find additional support through www.everythingEtsy.com/2009/06/20-ways-to-promote-your-Etsy-shop-with-discounts/.

CHAPTER 5

Why Marketing Outside Etsy is Important

W e've seen why marketing on Etsy is important. You can't just start your shop without building brand visibility. But after you've taken the trouble to promote yourself on Etsy, it's time to start promoting your Etsy shop to the rest of the Web. Doing so will build you a community of fans, followers and most importantly, shoppers.

GET YOUR WEB SITE AND BLOG UP AND RUNNING

So why do you need a Web site if you already have a store on Etsy? The answer is, you don't. But having a Web site allows you room for more content, such as your Etsy links, articles and blog posts. It also allows you to maintain a professional front, post more images, build your own forum or community messaging boards, and showcase all your various sites, blogs and social networking links under one roof.

Building a Web site is relatively easy, even if you don't have Web designer background. If you have some spare cash, it would be ideal to invest it in the services of an established Web designer, but even if you don't, you can still get a professional-looking site using free and readily available tools. The first thing you need to do is to select a Web-hosting company. These are generally not free services, but the costs are really affordable; www.bluehost. com starts at just $3.95 per month, while www. godaddy.com is $ 3.35 per month. They both include 24-hour customer service and have free tools that allow you to build your Web site in minutes. You can also download dozens of free applications like WordPress, Joomla and shopping carts (for selling products), and most of them will give you credits toward Google AdWords.

You can also check out Soopsee on www. soopsee.com. This site has over 100 Etsians already using it (http://www.soopsee.com/examples/) and it allows you to import your Etsy listings with a single click. You can import your blog, host your site on your own domain, use their huge library of graphics to personalize your site, and even upload charts and graphics that track your Etsy sales.

Another site that allows you to build your own Web site for free is www.webs.com. Once your site is built, link it to your Etsy shop in seconds with the Etsy application. Buyers who click on a product on your site are automatically taken to your Etsy shop from where the purchase is made. One of the major advantages is that it saves you the hassle of having to create a shopping cart on your site. And how easy (or difficult) is it to create your Web site? All you need is a bit of creativity and imagination and you're good to go. Most sites have really simple and ready to follow instructions, which take a matter of minutes to compete.

BUILDING A BLOG

Building a blog is easy and free, so why should you not take advantage of it and create your own special craft blog to promote your Etsy page? Although Twitter, Facebook and other social media networks can build a following for you, you can't own them and the content you post on them belongs to the site, not you. They are powerful tools to build relationships, but they are not the only tools. They are communication channels that lead back to your own core – your Web site and your blog.

Blogging can be one of the most effective marketing tools for the small business owner and home-based crafter. Blogs are easy to maintain and will do the following for your online store:

1. Deliver prospective customers to your doorstep

2. Supplement any other marketing you currently use

3. Test ideas via quizzes, polls or through comments received on posts

4. Build authority and make you a well-known figure in the craft community

5. Allow you to showcase your crafts

6. Get subscribers to your newsletter, ebook or any other additional services your site offers

7. Uncover new opportunities

But with the number of blogging platforms available, which one should you pursue? If you have your own Web site, use www.wordpress.org, because you can host it onto your own platform. It also has a lot of additional customized tools which are fun to play with and excellent to brand your blog. The following are a list of other blogging platforms, but note they are not self-hosted sites, but instead, sites which host your blog for you. Make a mistake and they can delete your content, leaving you to start from scratch. Having said this, a lot of businesses use them simply because they are extremely easy to set up.

BLOGGER

www.blogger.com is popular and free and is owned by Google. Best features? It can be set up in minutes and is really easy to use. It supports a lot of template editing, widget and application add-ons.

TUMBLR

www.tumblr.com has fused blogging and social networking to create an interesting result. The style used here is known as micro-blogging and the focus is on short and frequent content. Not ideal if you are not going to post regularly, but a good choice if you don't want the hassle of maintaining a blog full time.

TYPEPAD

www.typepad.com comes at a monthly or annual fee, which is based on the package selected. Different packages allow for varying storage space and customization options, and range from $8.95 per month to $14.95 per month. You can also get free trials to determine if TypePad is for you. The benefit to using TypePad is that it's easy to use, so you can get your blog up and running in moments. The downside to it is that you have the typepad.com extension to your blog, giving is a less professional appearance.

WORDPRESS

One of the most popular blogging platforms amongst crafters, www.wordpress.com is free and most Web-hosting sites will allow you to upload WordPress in an integrated fashion. You have an excellent choice of themes, applications, plug-ins, and gadgets. It's not as simple to set up as Blogger, but once you understand how to use it, it's an excellent choice as a blogging platform. WordPress also allows you to add and customize pages, so you can look at it as a Web site alternative.

Typically, you will find that WordPress offers easy customization, as well as hundreds of attractive templates. As an added bonus, if you do not like the way your site looks with one template, you can always change to a different one with a minimal amount of effort.

Having said this, as a one-man (or woman) craft creator, you might have certain reservations about the extra work a blog and Web site might create for you. The most common ones are the following:

1. **It's too expensive and difficult to create a Web site:** Ten years ago this might have been the case. But today, creating a Web site is as easy as a couple of clicks of the mouse. And for the expense, you can host a blog (free) and pay only for the plug-ins you choose, or you can go for a more traditional Web site through hosting companies like www.GoDaddy. com or www.Bluehost.com, which start as little as $3.50 per month. Use their Web-building tools to build your site for free. The templates and tools are so simple that even a beginner can create a site in an hour or so. But if you can't get your Web site built, you don't have to worry. Etsy is still the perfect place on which to showcase your wares.

2. **My business is too small to justify a Web site:** No business is too small to have an online presence. And if done correctly, a

small business has a fair chance of standing out and dominating the scene, like a large one. While craft stores usually have some products they can sell online, you don't have to have a product to be online. If you love to teach painting or knitting, you can market your teaching services online. Love to guide people as to where they can get the best supplies or ideas? Then how about setting up your own craft consulting business? All it takes is imagination and being online lets you achieve all that you dream of – and at times, even more.

3. **I don't have the time to update my Web site and blog:** Usually, once a Web site is created, the only thing which needs regular updates are your supplies or stores pages. These are the pages on which you might be offering new products on a regular basis. If you really find it hard to update these, you can always seek the services of a virtual assistant. Nowadays, there are a number of sites like www.vanetworking.com/ and www. virtualassistants.com/page2.html that, for a small fee, will update your site pages, add on blog content, and even take messages if you find yourself too busy to answer calls or check your email regularly.

If you still have reservations about why you should set up a blog, consider the following:

- Low costs to organize a marketing campaign compared to traditional methods

- Allows you to reach out to hundreds of customers and gives your business a national/global presence

- Allows your local clientele to shop from the comfort of their homes

- Keeps your store visible 24/7

- Allows you to test new products, services and markets in smaller targeted campaigns

- Gives your customers a chance to type in instant customer feedback, which is an integral part of any marketing campaign

- Allows you to make your campaign an interactive one, where you can actually communicate one on one with your customer

- Gives you the opportunity to promote time-sensitive campaigns, very useful when you want to unload stock or require immediate funds

DRIVE TRAFFIC TO YOUR BLOG

So you've decided to build a blog and have selected a blogging platform. The first thing you want to do is have all the content you put on this site link back to your Etsy store. This can be done by inserting links within the post or by creating a signature at the end of each piece, which has your Etsy store links to it. This ensures all your visitors will click on the link and be directed back to your Etsy site. Or you can put your Etsy store link to the side of your blog under the heading 'My Etsy Store' or something equally pronounced.

Later we'll see how to create valuable content; but first, let's see how we can drive traffic to your blog.

1. Set up an email subscription from your own blog, and invite friends, family members and others in your craft network to subscribe to it. You can also add the subscription link to your Web site so you can cross-promote it.

2. Visit other craft sites and comment intelligently on them. You can't expect other crafting enthusiasts to visit your site if you simply say things like "nice blog" on their sites. Show them you've taken the trouble to read through their posts. If you're stuck for time, visit one different site per day rather

than trying to cram more in. Plus, this way you'll have the chance to get to know seven new sites each week.

3. Ping your posts. www.pingomatic.com is a wonderful site that allows you to share your blog's content each time fresh material is posted.

4. Visit ezine directories like www.ezinearticles. com or www.goarticles.com and submit fresh content to them. When it comes to promoting Web sites, almost every Webmaster spends a significant amount of time submitting articles to directors. For example, ezinearticles.com, ehow.com, goarticles.com, and isnare.com all tend to receive an enormous amount of traffic from people that are looking for various kinds of information. While Webmasters do not get paid for submissions to these sites, the back links tend to be very valuable. In fact, you may be surprised to find that a significant amount of traffic to your site will often coincide with article directory submissions.

During the process of submitting articles to directories, it is also important to realize that other people will come along and place your articles on their Web sites. Typically, most directories will allow this to occur as long as the person using the content links back to your site. Invariably, this will boost your number of back links, as well as keep your content flowing around the Internet. At the same time, your content will most often be picked up by individuals who are blogging or developing Web sites about related items. Since the site linking to yours will be relevant, these back links will be even more valuable in terms of search engine ranking.

If you are going to submit articles to directories, you will need to make sure that you can deliver interesting information. Even though many authors try to be authoritative, it is important to realize that your viewers all have different personalities. Therefore, what you may see as authoritative may seem overbearing or dictatorial to someone else. As an artist trying to appeal to the emotions of your viewers, it may be better to take a softer approach. Interestingly enough, the most successful article marketers tend to draw from personal experience. Even though it is not always necessary to write in the first tense, you may find that it will help you focus your thoughts.

As a general rule of thumb, you will need to make daily submissions to at least five or six article directories in order to gain and then maintain a reasonable level of traffic. If you are trying to design and manufacture jewelry, you may not have the time, let alone the energy to do all of that writing.

Fortunately, there are many writers available online that will perform this task for a fee. You may also want to let them submit the articles on your behalf

And finally, remember that all directories allow you a short site/author description, so craft one that generates interest and draws visitors to your Etsy store.

5. **Set up an RSS feed on your blog post** so visitors can subscribe to consequent posts. Don't forget you are still linking to your Etsy store in all your posts.

6. **Create regular content for your site.** Once you begin to blog, consistency is the key to growing your fan base. For the most part, you should plan on creating at least one blog post per day. This will ensure that content is being added to your site on a regular basis. And it's not only your fans who will appreciate it. Search engine spiders that crawl the Web looking for fresh material will be thrilled to see your new and updated content, giving your blog a better rank. And a better rank usually translates into a bigger audience.

When it comes to your blogging schedule, you may also want to give some thought to when you will actually write them. Unlike live postings to the

Etsy.com Web site, you can always choose to write your blogs all at once, and then simply post them on another date. When you use the WordPress or Blogger platform, you can simply upload them in bulk, and then keep them in draft mode until you are ready to publish them.

7. **Write title tags that are search engine attractive.** These are generally short, snappy, and contain keywords that are designed to draw traffic to your site. You can write your tag and then check at Overture, WordTracker or KeyWordDiscovery to see how well it does and modify it accordingly.

8. **Participate in blog forums and on community sites.** Etsy community forums are a great place to get started, but expand your search to other craft forums. Visit www. technorati.com to check out the forums that apply to your line of crafts and then begin frequenting them.

9. **Link to other posts**, but do so carefully. Linking can be very constructive when done correctly. Target the craft sites you want to be associated with and include them in your posts. The same holds true of suppliers and other related artisans. Also know that if you

quote other crafters or use information from their site, as a matter of etiquette, you should link to them.

10. And last, but definitely not least, **invite guest bloggers to write on your blog**. Asking a well-known personality to share his/her advice can prove invaluable in taking your blog from "friends and family" readership to a much wider audience. A small note on guest bloggers: make sure they agree to provide their posts in advance and are OK with you editing them. Remember, it's your blog and your style, so ensure content posted on it fits in. While you will link to your guest blogger's site, don't forget to continue to include your Etsy store in the post.

CUSTOMER TESTIMONIALS AND CUSTOMER PHOTOS

Once you start selling your craft online, it is very important to find out how your customers feel about their purchase. And if you know they like your work, you can always ask for testimonials to publish on your blog. In fact, if you ask customers for permission to feature their story or insights on your blog, they may develop into loyal fans.

If you are going to feature customer testimonials, try also to obtain photos. When it comes to testimonials, nothing speaks better than an image of a customer wearing your created jewelry or sporting your designed bag.

It may take some time before you can find customers that will give you a testimonial. Their presence will be a sure sign that your business is well on the way to being a success. As an added bonus, when viewers visit your blog, these testimonials can easily encourage readers to visit your Etsy.com store.

Unfortunately, there are unscrupulous merchants that will create false testimonials and photos in order to make their offerings look more attractive. Interestingly enough, most potential customers have a sixth sense when it comes to spotting these kinds of sites. As may be expected, potential customers will avoid these sellers as much as possible. You're better off not having any testimonials than having fake ones.

KEEP YOUR READERS COMING BACK

While you may publish postings to your blog on a daily basis, readers will lose interest if you do not provide them with something special to attract their attention. Typically, the best thing you can do is create a timely post. For example, you may want to post information about a local fashion show that you will be hosting. Even though your customers may be located on the other side of the world, they will still be interested in seeing pictures from the event.

Today, many bloggers use contests, raffles and mystery newsbreaks to ensure viewers will return to their blog on a regular basis. Chances are, you can come up with several other marketing campaigns to attract attention. For example, if you often visit social networking sites, you will find plenty of people that offer freebies to site visitors. Invariably, if you feature something of a similar nature on your site, you are sure to generate a good bit of traffic.

PROVIDE VALUABLE AND UNIQUE WEB CONTENT

When it comes to gaining viewership, one of the most important aspects of attracting customers to your site is to provide them with valuable content.

Valuable content can be in the form of an audio MP3 message, a YouTube video, or most commonly, written material.

While most Web site owners are quick to provide content, with the increasing importance of SEO (search engine optimization), they are selecting their keywords based on ranking and potential revenue. While it's important to keep SEO in mind, it's even more important to understand that your article, Web content, newsletter or press release should be drafted based on the value it can provide to your audience. Keywords can be used, but they should be integrated around the article, not the article around them.

In order for you to gain visitors to your Etsy craft site, to be a leader in what you do, and to make your brand stand out from your competitors, you do need to provide incredible value to your audience. When writing your article or Web site content, check to see it does the following:

- **Educates**
- **Entertains**
- **Enlightens**

No one is more appreciative of getting free and valuable advice that your readers. If you can provide them with resources for suppliers, tips on how to get their own craft going, or ideas they can use in creating their craft, they are going to be happy to reciprocate by visiting your site, buying your books and products, and signing up for your courses.

You do not have to be a great writer to provide good content, but you do have to be good communicator. When you write, check to see if your tone of voice is easy to follow. Are you being natural? Do you speak in the same language as your audience? Is your advice simple and easy to follow? Can they understand the words you use?

Be yourself and write in the same voice you use to speak, using clear and simple words to convey your message.

There are plenty of places you can **source ideas from**, such as ezine directories, magazines, press releases, newspapers, television news, Yahoo, Google and Bing search engines, social networking sites, and even by chatting with other craft enthusiasts. Keep a book handy and jot down ideas as they come to you. When you need them, go through the book and select the ones that make the most sense in the context of the message you are trying to convey. Use your life experiences to tell a story. All readers love a good story.

When writing an article, be it for a blog or ezine directory, if you are stuck for ideas, the following will help:

How-to guides: These are articles that contain valuable resources, such as information on how to upload your craft on Etsy, how to set up your own bead-making business, or how to organize a craft room.

Lists: Lists are also very popular and can be a simple as, "10 Sites Where You Can Market Your Crafts" or "Top 10 Suppliers for Paper Crafts."

Questions: A question and answer format also works well as most readers do have questions, such as, "How do I stick a thin border on correctly?" Or, "How can I decorate with decoupage?"

Give a benefit: An example here could be the benefit of using varnish on your beads, or why a clear desk can produce a higher output.

Define something: By defining something you are suggesting to your audience they can gain answers just by reading the text or watching the video.

Write a headline that arouses curiosity. "Seven Ways to Use Dried Flowers in Your Home" is a great heading because it gets people curious. Most can imagine one or two ways, not seven, so they will read on to find out what they are.

Tying in to current events is also a good way to draw in the crowd. Browse through Etsy's site to see what everyone is talking about and use this to craft your article. Similarly, if a celebrity has recently been in the news for her beaded couture bag and you produce beaded bags, link the story to your article. It will give it more weight.

Spice up your article with images from your own work or by using image from sites like Stock. XCHNG (www.sxc.hu) or FreeImages (www. freeimages.co.uk/).

Stick to the point. If it's a how-to article or a question and answer article, ensure you work within the framework. If you want an informal blog with ramblings of your visit to the farm or what your kitten played with today, then you need to redefine your blog and social networking content. You will draw a wide audience, but the majority will be from one group or the other – so cater to their needs first.

Reward your visitors. If you do want to draw visitors to your Etsy store (the entire point of this ebook), consider giving them a bonus by way of a free ebook, a discount on your products, a buy-one-get-one-free offer, or a sales price for your products.

If you are still stuck for ideas or time to create your own articles, you can republish articles from article directory sites, and give credit to other authors. However, it's not recommended to do this frequently as it draws visitors away from your own craft site to other craft sites. Also note that as the quality varies drastically, you can use them to gain ideas rather than copy them word for word. Most of them will have publisher's terms of use, so be sure to read them carefully before downloading the articles.

COMMUNICATING VIA VIDEOS

Videos, slideshows, and PowerPoint presentations are a great way to communicate with an audience, build up a following and become an authority in your craft field. If you don't want to produce your own videos, don't worry, you can also upload related videos to your blog from YouTube. Both blogger and WordPress allow you to do this in a few simple steps.

CREATING A YOUTUBE VIDEO

If you are daring and want to go ahead with creating a YouTube video, here are six easy steps to do so:

1. Create your free YouTube account and don't forget to check the terms of service.

2. Make a short movie using a digital camera, Web camera, or even a phone (though ensure the latter produces good quality videos). In the next section we outline what kind of videos you can make.

3. Edit your movie using Window's Moviemaker.

4. Resize the video so it fits into the YouTube frame correctly. YouTube also has a 100MB and 10-minute limit.

5. Enter your YouTube account and click on the link: Upload Videos.

6. Create your title, description and tags, which will help people find your video. Don't forget to mention your Etsy store in both the description and on the video.

You're now good to go!

COMMUNICATING VIA
MP3 RECORDINGS

For those who don't like to be recorded on video cameras, consider using an MP3 message on your Web site and blog. This is a fun way of telling people who you are, talking about your Etsy craft store, and inviting visitors to have a look at it. Most Web-hosting companies allow you to upload MP3 recordings, but some do have a space limit, so check with your Web-hosting company before you create and upload one.

OPTIMIZE WEB CONTENT

Traffic from search engines is considered the best way to generate traffic back to your site, and this can be done cost effectively by using what are known as keywords.

Keywords, however, can be tricky to think up by yourself, so it's great to have tools at hand to help you generate them. You can use inexpensive and free services, including Google AdWords (www. adwords.google.com/), HowRank (www.howrank. com/Keywords-Rocket-Tool.php) and Wordtracker (www.wordtracker.com/).

During the process of finding blog topics, you should always give some thought to keyword optimization. If your blog posts are not targeted to jewelry, for example, you may find that search engines will not index it properly. This, in turn, will make it harder to attract an audience that may be interested in buying jewelry.

At the very least, you should keep a list of 15 to 20 keywords on hand at all times. Even if you dedicate one post to each keyword, you will be ensuring that your blog is relevant to your target audience. As an added bonus, when you are having difficulty choosing a topic, using a keyword can help you focus a bit faster on something that can be developed into a full post.

Here are some key ways to optimize your sites, articles and online newsletters:

1. **Target one word for each page**. This is opposed to stuffing each page with keywords, which – at the very least – can get your site banned.

2. **List your keywords in links**. This way when someone uses your links on their sites, your keyword is taken into consideration.

3. **Make your first 100 words in your Web copy keyword-rich** as this is what most search engines target. Remember this would

include your menu, if your menu is located on the left hand side.

4. **Insert keywords into your title tag**, which in code are 'header tags,' or 'meta tags.' Also include them into your keyword tags.

5. **Place your keywords in your header**. This would be a selected keyword for each header you use in all your articles.

6. **Enrich your word copy.** A good keyword density is around 3 percen to 5 percent, so aim for this. Also keep the body text short and concise, so you can add fresh new content more frequently.

Even though it may seem like creating, and maintaining, a blog appears to be a lot of work, don't worry. Once you create and optimize your blog properly, it will run automatically. Many people enjoy maintaining a blog because they like sharing with an audience and they like seeing a community grow amongst the regular readers. Who knows? You may come to enjoy blogging as much as you do creating crafts. And if your buyers can sense your enjoyment, they will be that much more interested in purchasing your wares.

CHAPTER SIX

Building a Mailing List to Keep in Touch with Your Buyers (and Fans)

Y ou have your blog, you have your networking community – the next step is to grow this community and build your mailing list. To do so, you will need to employ list-building strategies. The basis of these strategies is to build trust and to establish relationships. Once you have your list, you can do almost anything with it; craft a newsletter to inform your readers about new products, special sales offers, promotional items, new social media sites you've joined, etc; sell affiliate products or sell your own products.

THE FIRST TWO RULES TO REMEMBER ARE:

1. Building a list takes a lot of time and can't be rushed.

2. Free lists don't exist and paid-for lists are usually unreliable.

The biggest mistake most business owners make is not starting their list from day one. The best time to set up your list is the day you set up your blog. The longer you wait, the harder it gets and you stand to lose more potential customers.

Begin by selecting the right email marketing software. The reason for this is that U.S. law requires a client to sign up to a list in order to be considered 'subscribed.' If he doesn't sign up and you continue to send mail to his email address, it's considered spam and is a punishable offense.

Secondly, when you switch from one email host provider to another, you can lose up to 80 percent of subscribers on your list! Imagine even if you have a small list of 100 names and lose 80 of them! As mentioned earlier, it takes a long time to build a list and this list really is valuable. So take care when selecting the right provider.

While there are a host of autoresponder or email software providers, the top two are Aweber (www.aweber.com) and Constant Contact (www. constantcontact.com) Select either of them and you should be fine. Remember, if you are switching between them, your subscribers will still need to opt in, so go through both Web sites before you make a decision. Neither is free, but they offer a lot more value than the free sites do. Aweber allows you to test its site for $1 for the first month, so take advantage of this special offer.

Now that you have email software for your list, the next step is to capture leads. A lead is generally captured via a sign-up box, which you can install for free on your blog or Web site. Most small business owners, craft stores included, tend to have a single sign-up box and leave it at that. But multiple sign-up boxes (all free) increase your chance to capturing multiple leads, so try and use them wherever possible – your Web site, blog, newsletter and any other online marketing material you use.

Your sign up box is a standard visible box that explains what you are offering and how the reader can get it. It's usually placed in a highly visible section, to the top of your marketing material, so it attracts the reader right away. Some services like Aweber offer what is known as a 'pop-up box,' which is a sign-up window that pops up when the site is entered. A lot of readers find that it's intrusive, though there is a 'close' button that easily gets rid of it. You can fill in a lot more information on a 'pop-up' box than you can on a sign-up box. You can also use it to showcase a piece of your best craft, which will attract more visitors to sign up. Another option is to select a 'footbox' ad, which is like a pop-up box, but is less intrusive as it appears at the footer of the page. The best way to find out which one best suits your business is to try both of them and test them with a small audience.

Another way to capture leads is by sending an email out to those who comment on your blog post. A simple email response can be built in to your autoresponder. Include a thank you and an offer to receive a free ebook or discount on any sales made at your site. They simply click on the autoresponder link, which in turn gives you their name and email address.

You will also get great marketing leads from Facebook. Simple add a sign-up box to your fan page.

There are many reasons it's worth it to work so hard to capture leads. It's hard to build a relationship with your readers if you do not communicate with them on a more personal basis, and your lead-generating tools allow you to do just that. Build up a relationship and it's so much easier to direct them back to your Etsy store for more sales. The autoresponder is a relationship-building tool that helps place your brand in the spotlight, makes you an authority in the craft you create, and builds up reader trust – all necessities when you sell online.

Setting up an autoresponder is extremely easy and the only difficult part might be finding content to send out on a regular basis. Refer to the ways to find content for your blog post in the earlier section, and apply the same to creating content for your newsletter.Just remember: the ultimate goal for all this work is to send traffic to your Etsy Store, so ensure all your newsletters or messages that go out through your autoresponder have your Etsy Store link on them.

LIST-BUILDING ESSENTIALS

Before you begin to send emails to potential subscribers, you need to be sure you are following the next three rules:

RULE #1

ASK PERMISSION

Anti-spam laws require that you ask for permission before you send out any email. Failure to follow these laws is punishable and can get your site bookmarked as a spam-sending site, so be careful how and to whom you send emails. This is one reason buying direct mailing lists doesn't work. Take the above recommendations – send an automated email to your new social networking contacts and to those who comment on your site – and build your list in a credible and correct manner. This is called permission-based email marketing, and it works.

RULE #2

TAKE IMMEDIATE ACTION

Don't wait too long before asking permission to add a potential subscriber onto your list. If the customer gives you her email, she expects to see something in her inbox fairly soon. It takes a second to insert her name and email into your automated email list, so do it before distractions overtake you and the customer is forgotten.

RULE #3

INSERT DOUBLE OPT-IN AND OPT-OUT LINKS

A double opt-in link means the customer is asked permission before his name is added to your list, and he has to confirm, usually by clicking on a link. In doing so, his name is then directly added. This prevents any misunderstandings and/or frauds, and the customer is assured no one else can add his name without his permission. Some stores believe a double opt-in makes for more work for the customer. But, as it's a simple link he has to click on before he receives further information or a confirmation email, most customers are happy to do it. They feel the list they are subscribing to is more secure.

Similarly, give them permission to opt out of or unsubscribe from the subscriber list if they want to. While some of them may do so, you can also provide them with a box for their comments. This way the client is assured he's not stuck with something he doesn't want, and you get feedback from him that you can use to improve your site. Also, remember these rules are not just about good customer service; they are also the law.

STILL MORE WAYS TO BUILD UP YOUR SUBSCRIBER LIST

While putting a lead-generator form on your Web site and blog may generate most of your subscribers, there are other ways you'll need to explore to gain new names for your list. Marketing is an ongoing process that builds up momentum if done regularly.

But the moment you stop, you are in danger of not only losing this momentum (and having to start from scratch), but also losing customers subscribed to your list. If you do not provide quality content (see above for ways to generate content) and if you do not provide regular content, subscribers are happy to move to someone who does.

Here are some great places in which to add your lead generator box or sign-up link:

1. In your newsletter

Just because your newsletter goes out to your subscribers, doesn't mean you stop promoting it. If you do send out a regular email, add a sign-up link to your newsletter with a request to forward it if the customer feels someone else might enjoy it. Think about this – if your newsletter does get forwarded and the person receiving it doesn't know how to subscribe, you have immediately lost a potential client. If you don't have a sign-up box, continue to add your link to all outgoing messages.

A NOTE ABOUT NEWSLETTERS

Email newsletters can be effective tools to market your Etsy store. In order to get people to keep subscribing to your newsletter and recommend it to their friends and colleagues, remember to ensure your newsletter is:

1. **Short** and to the point: No one enjoys reading long emails.

2. **Well designed**: Don't add too many graphics, colors or fonts. Make sure your email is simple to read, visually pleasing and opens well in all types of email readers such as Yahoo mail, Gmail and Outlook.

3. **Professional**: People want advice from professionals, so offer valuable and true content. If a project is hard to create, explain at the outset the skills required to follow it.

The vast majority of online merchants will tell you that mailing lists are absolutely necessary if you expect to generate a reasonable volume of sales. In fact, some merchants will tell you that as much as 50 percent of their revenue is generated by sending out emails on a regular basis. Even if a viewer has not purchased from your site, sending emails will help to gain further attention from them. At the very least, if someone is willing to give you their email address, then you know you have already gained some attention from them.

When you are going to send an email to potential customers, the worst thing you can do is send them a flyer filled with prices and pictures. Behavior offline tends to be duplicated online. Do you read every single flyer that appears in your mailbox? Chances are, you probably do not even bother to read ones from supermarkets that you shop at on a regular basis. Unfortunately, sending just one flyer to potential customers may be enough to ensure that they mark your mailings as spam.

Today, most online marketers use a number of other methods to make sales pitches. In particular, newsletters, mini-courses and email blogging are very popular. Since weekly and monthly posting tends to be an ideal saturation level, you may want to start out with a newsletter. Even though the content of the newsletter should not be a duplication of your blog, you can still recycle facts and information presented on the site. In fact, you can easily send a weekly newsletter that acts as a summary of your blog.

NEWSLETTER CONTENT
THAT WORKS

When someone suspects that you are making a sales pitch, they will already be inclined to avoid your emails. Therefore, when you create newsletters, you will need to be very careful about the placement of sales pitches. It is also very important to choose content for your newsletter that will ensure readers will be eager to read the next one.

As an owner of a craft store, there are a number of topics that might work in your favor. These include talking about new designs that you are working on. In fact, if you have a loyal following, then you may want to offer an exclusive newsletter that will include discounts or other bonuses.

If you are having problems generating newsletter content, you may want to also sign up for newsletters created by other online merchants. Even if you do not choose newsletters dedicated to jewelry, you can still study them in order to learn more about newsletter structure and subject selection. As can be expected, if you are interested in learning more about your competitors, signing up for their newsletters will give you a number of insights.

2. Via social networking sites and blogs

This has already been covered, but it's important to know that any new site or blog you network on should also carry your message loud and clear. Insert your email address, Etsy store link, or lead generator box where possible.

3. On your business card

Add a direct link to your sign-up box or to your Web site with a mention of what you want them to sign up for. For example. "Sign up to receive my free monthly newsletter!"

4. At craft fairs and networking events

If you are exchanging cards at craft fairs or other networking events, ask permission to add people you meet to your subscriber list.

5. On all printed material your store generates

This could include the bags or boxes you use to mail out your crafts, the invoices you send, the brochures you create for the store, and the advertising you elect to undertake. Include an incentive to get people to respond immediately, such as: "Sign up to our free newsletter and get a chance to win a necklace in our monthly drawing."

6. On all outgoing messages

Your signature can be a powerful tool to attract visitors to your site, immediately. Use a clear and legible font, and keep your message brief. Invite people to visit your Etsy store and sign up for your newsletter at the given link.

7. At meetings and conferences

Just like at craft fairs and networking groups, meetings and conferences are a great place to invite people to visit your Etsy site and sign up for your newsletter. Keep simple, one-page brochures or printed sheets on hand to distribute to potential customers. Again, incentives work really well, so give away something by way of a drawing or door prize.

8. At your store or craft fair table

If you have your own brick and mortar store or table at a craft fair or Sunday market, consider having a sign-up sheet next to the register. You can print out a color copy of your newsletter as a visual aid so viewers can see it and sign up immediately. Again, consider offering an incentive – a small discount that they can use toward their next purchase. This ensures they agree to subscribe once you've sent them their double opt-in confirmation link. Remember to send them the link immediately.

9. In your author box

Write articles for ezine directories? Act as a guest blogger on other Web sites? Your author box is a powerful way to describe you and your craft, and to get visitors to view your Etsy store. Invite them to join your subscriber list and provide a link. Some ezine directories do not allow you to have more than one link, so you might need to word your message carefully and consolidate all your links – subscriber link, Etsy store link, Web site link and blog link – into a single page they can access.

10. By joining forums and discussion boards

It's difficult to hard-sell your newsletter on forums and discussion boards, and it's considered rude to do so. It may also result in your Web site getting banned. Having said that, it's been included in this list because it's a strong tool if used correctly. By correctly, what one means is that a forum is a place for fun and intelligent discussion. By participating in one regularly, you get your name and brand noticed, making it easier to promote your Etsy store indirectly. The same rules of social media participation apply here; be consistent, provide value, visit other forum members' sites and comment intelligently on them. If there's just one site you must select, Google your craft and research the forums that pop up. Or you could consider joining a site like Creating The Hive (http://creatingthehive.com).

USE YOUR LIST EFFECTIVELY

One of the big reasons you'll be growing a list is to market your Etsy store effectively. You can send out sales information, new product information and ask people to help you promote your store by recommending it to others. But there are other reasons to build your list as well. You can diversify your marketing and tap into different streams of income – and relate them all back to your Etsy store. Here are just a few ways to do this:

1. **Affiliate marketing**: Affiliate marketing works two ways: you can sell other craft items and gain a commission from them (sign on to sites like www.clickbank.com to begin) or you can pay affiliate marketers (who earn a commission off each of your sales) to promote your Etsy store. The latter works well only if you can sell in volume or if you have high-priced pieces.

2. **One-on-one teaching**: Do you specialize in something so unique that others would love to learn from you? You can set up your own online teaching classes and promote them via your mailing list.

3. **Group coaching**: If one-on-one teaching is not to your liking, how about a group

coaching session? Depending on what craft you specialize in, you can teach through Webinars or precreated videos.

4. **eBooks**: Writing and selling ebooks on your craft is always a great option and you can create one with little or no overhead (but you do need to invest time to make sure it reads well). Turn it into a PDF and load it onto your Web site. You can begin by selling it to your list.

These are only a few ways to make your list work for you. You will use it to continue to promote your Etsy store and draw visitors back to your site. If you work at building a mailing list, and use it effectively, it can be a powerful thing. Often times, people will announce a sale or a unique offer only to their list. Within a day or two an influx of sales comes from those subscribed to your list. Taking a few minutes to write an email is about as easy—and free—as marketing ideas go.

CHAPTER SEVEN

Even More Ways to Market Your Craft Business

Your network consists of both your support system and your business income. It is those members – friends, family, current customers and potential customers – who will give you advice, take your advice, buy from you and recommend your products/ services to others. Without an online network, your business cannot grow. And the key to growing your network is simple and threefold: a) join social media sites; b) build your mailing list; and c) use your list effectively.

JOIN SOCIAL MEDIA SITES

Join as many networking channels as you effectively can, the keyword being effective. If you sign up to a network, social media or otherwise, you need to market yourself on it consistently. Doing any less will be a waste of time and effort. There's a lot of talk about how social media networking is important, but unfortunately, most of us are going around doing it the incorrect way. Social media is not for making sales – it's for building a network, which leads to sales. It's a place for being yourself, sharing your values, your beliefs in your crafts and in how they can help others. Social media, if used correctly, can be an effective tool that turns your followers into potential buyers.

But most social media training you find online is outdated and works around single models. Your craft business is a specific, individual tool that needs to be shaped accordingly. And you can do so in **four simple steps** without having to pay big bucks to online marketing gurus to do so. Here's what you need to do to grow your network:

STEP 1

BRAND YOURSELF AROUND YOUR PASSION

In this case, it's your craft business. But even if you are a one-man (or woman) show, you have got to think of yourself as a brand leader in what you do. You are the brand and the brand is you. It's a lifelong asset that gives you satisfaction and a bank balance. You need to step up as a brand leader, offering advice that makes you and, by default, your brand, well known in the marketplace. Is your passion about making homemade jams? Can you share this knowledge with others through your blog? Can your company, *Jam With Jemma* tweet about the various summer fruit to include in your jams? There's so much you can do if you remember to be proactive and consistent.

STEP 2

DO YOUR RESEARCH

Before hopping onto the social media band-wagon, do your research carefully. Where do all the jam-lovers hide? Are there any culinary sites you can join that will double your exposure? Is LinkedIn really going to help your business at this stage? Your ideal audience is going to be comprised of people just like you – who share your likes and sometimes dislikes, and more importantly, who love to cook and bake.

STEP 3

CHOOSE A PRIMARY FOCUS

Don't dilute your brain. If you love to make jams and making beaded barrettes, figure out which one is going to be your primary focus. When two crafts are somewhat related – for example, making beaded barrettes and making bracelets – it's simple to clump them together and market them both to the sites and audience you select. But when one is completely unrelated to another, your marketing tactics need to be revised. Jams for Jemma then can't include barrettes, unless you want to promote them as a 'Buy two jams and get one hand-made barrette for FREE."

STEP 4

KEEP THE PASSION ALIVE

Sometimes it's hard to be brave when you have not made a single sale on your Etsy store. You've been blogging, tweeting and redirecting customers to your Etsy site, but the results have been less than satisfactory. And it's so easy to give up and ignore your blog and social networking accounts. Remember, social networking is not about making sales, it's about building a network which will translate into sales. But this translation can take time. The trick is to use any downtime you have to build your brand up. Focus on spending free time to blog even more, send more articles to ezine directories, and get your brand out there. The results can come only with a consistent effort.

POPULAR SOCIAL NETWORKING SITES
THAT CRAFTERS ON ETSY USE:

TWITTER

Twitter is a platform that allows users to send short messages (140 characters) called "tweets" to their followers. It's an ideal tool to network with those who share your interests, and to promote your crafts and handmade items. The best part of Twitter is that it allows you to type these messages from your Web site, via an automated program such as www.socialoomph.com or even via a cell phone using mobile apps. You can build your business 24/7 by being visible to millions of people online, and you can grow your own following simply by deciding on how active, and proactive, you want to be. You have only 160 characters for your profile, so ensure you make it memorable and include your Etsy link. Then, select a custom background, which makes a big difference in how people view your business. A collage of your products might make for an interesting theme and sites like www.picasa.com allow you to build them from your online album. You can upload your newly created theme directly to Twitter as a backdrop.

Now that you've done this, sign up to a site like socialoomph.com and tweet for the next 10 days.

Don't make all of them business related. Include any favorite sites you've come across, links that others might find interesting, headlines from the latest in the crafting world and even jokes and quotes, if appropriate.

Tweet your blog posts directly by using a WordPress-created theme, or if you are not on WordPress, then sites like Twitterfeed will allow you to link your blog post directly to your Twitter account. Write a new post and it automatically shows up on Twitter.

Don't forget to mingle with the folks online. This is a great chance to get to know others in the business. Just type a topic in the search box to the right of your Twitter feed and you'll find hundreds and thousands of names you can select from.

Launching a new line? A new product? Made some big sales? It's not only OK to talk about them on Twitter, it's expected. Let others share in your joy when you close a big deal with your local arts and crafts center, or buy from your store when you announce a big "one day only" sale. Remember not to flood your page with sales and offers. Let your readers breathe in between and give them a chance to make a decision, forward an announcement, or comment on a topic.

FACEBOOK

According to recent statistics, nearly 200 million users are on Facebook with a million users joining each week in the U.S. alone. Facebook users are across the world with a wide range of demographics – from single mothers looking to socialize, to teenagers, friends, business executives and most certainly, business owners. For the latter in particular, Facebook is an excellent tool by which to grow your business and here's how:

Create a memorable profile: Strong and powerful profiles are important for any online presence –on Etsy, your Web site, blog or Facebook. Creating this section is free and there's plenty of space to describe you and your business, so spend some time on filling in the details.

Build up your contact list: The entire purpose of Facebook is to connect with friends, family members, and in the case of your craft business, potential buyers, suppliers and distributors. Newer opportunities can arise via a site like Facebook, but to take advantage of them, you need to network extensively. The ability to connect with friends' friends is also a powerful application that will enable you to build your network.

Send messages: Once you connect, don't leave it there. Send out a friendly message to say hello, tell them who you are and what you do, and invite them to view your Etsy store page. If you have an ezine or newsletter, it's also a good opportunity to invite them to sign up for it.

Post wall messages: Short messages are great to announce a sale or a special limited-time offer. Wall messages are also a good way to say hello and respond to messages posted by others in the group.

Build a fan page: Facebook also allows you to build and brand a company page where you can have links back to your Etsy store, post wall messages for all who 'like' your site to see, send out group messages and invite your audience into a discussion – all great ways to build a larger, interactive community interested in what you have to offer.

Participate in groups: By adding favorite groups to your site and participating in them, you can network with a lot of other craft companies and update your knowledge about what's happening. You can also sign on to Etsy's product page or the Everything Etsy site. To reach them, simply type Etsy into the search box.

Update your status: And finally, if you find it hard to manage your Facebook account, as it can be quite time-consuming and you can get sidetracked, simply take it upon yourself to update your status frequently and reserve an hour once a week to respond to the messages you receive. It's that simple!

TWO OTHER POINTS TO NOTE ABOUT FACEBOOK

There is an application that allows buyers to 'gift' your products to someone else.

You can advertise on Facebook, which in a lot of cases can be cheaper than advertising across Google's AdWords. The ads are short, but you can upload an image, so select wisely and don't forget to add your Etsy store link.

YOUTUBE

While YouTube was once considered a place to post silly videos about your dog and its antics, it's emerged as an excellent and cost-effective business tool by which to promote your craft business. You can use it to show off your own expertise via demonstrations, market your products and connect with a wider range of customers from around the world.

You can also host short interviews and invite guest crafters to be on the video with you. In fact, in doing so, you are automatically associating yourself with a more successful brand, which in turn boosts your own brand.

Not comfortable about creating a video of yourself doing a craft demonstration? Then how about creating a slideshow that works as a step-by-step guide. www.picasa.com, for example, is a great site to convert your images into a slideshow and add written content.

And if you have customers who've loved your work, include them in your videos. Who says client testimonials have to be bland and boring written comments? There's nothing more impactful that having a client wear a piece of your jewelry or your hand-painted shawl while speaking about your work!

You will market yourself on YouTube the same way you market yourself on any other networking community – subtly and consistently. Leaving well-thought-out comments, visiting others' sites and inviting users back to your site will all have a positive effect in directing visitors to your store. Add your YouTube URL to all your marketing material, including Facebook, blogs, email signatures and Web site profiles. In addition, embed your created videos on your Web site, blog or other social networking site pages.

You might also consider reciprocal videos – i.e. place your creations onto someone else's video (e.g.

your handbags in a clothes designer's show) for a link to the video placed on your blog or Web site. Since you have a noncompeting common goal, pooling resources will always create a mutual advantage.

To summarize, here are a few ways you can use YouTube to effectively market your Etsy Store:

- Upload a short video demonstration
- Invite a guest crafter to do a demonstration
- Conduct an interview
- Upload a slideshow
- Invite customers to give their testimonials online

When you create your video or slideshow, don't forget that branding is all-important. Select a user name that reflects your brand (or you can use your brand name itself).

It is important to realize that YouTube is owned by Google. Interestingly enough, if you do a keyword search on just about any phrase, the Google search engine will always provide links to relevant videos ahead of Web site results.

If you want to capture a top spot in the Google search engine, crafting noteworthy videos will be of immense benefit.

LINKEDIN

LinkedIn is another way to promote your business, and while it often gives the impression of being more suitable for corporations or bus-iness executives, the fact is, even a home-based business can benefit greatly from being on LinkedIn. It's a rapidly growing network with over 65 million members on it, and like all the other social networking sites outlined in this section, it's free to join, which makes it relatively inexpensive to include in your marketing plan.

Signing on is simple and once you provide your profile and upload your picture, you are ready to go. LinkedIn has a lot of unique features, but the one that stands out the most is the recommendation button. Use this to have customers recommend you. While this might not always be in direct reference to a particular craft, it still is an excellent testimony to your company and to your professionalism as a business owner and it certainly builds up credibility for your business.

Remember, the more optimized your profile, the better your chances of it being picked up by search engines like Google. LinkedIn has strong rankings on Google.

Also, make use of subtle features that enhance your ranking, such as changing 'my blog' by default, to the name of your blog.

Continue to build up contacts first through friends and customers, and as your networking skills grow, to a wider audience who might be interested in your work. You can use the LinkedIn search button to begin your search for people who are on the same network.

NING NETWORK

While Twitter and Facebook are extremely popular with social networkers, there's another network that's gaining popularity and it's called Ning. Relatively new, Ning recently announced they've reached over 37 million users with over 1.6 million social networks created. That's right, Ning allows businesses to create their own social network which is highly effective when it comes to brand building. Their service is free, and a paid-for premium option allows users to create their own domain name and use additional promotional apps to build and promote their site.

On Ning you can create your own profile page to showcase your Etsy store, you can add friends, send and receive messages and update your status on a regular basis. Use it effectively for the following:

- Build your own community and get feedback and opinions from current customers as well as potential buyers.

- Start creative discussions about your craft and your products, which need not be restricted to your customers, but can expand to the community around you.

- Customize your Ning site by yourself or with the aid of a Web design company in keeping with your branding. It's also easy to install third party apps if needed.

- Publish a detailed profile of yourself and your work, which you can use for all the Ning sites you join.

- Publish a blog, which is another great feature to bear in mind.

Visit www.ning.com and type "Arts and Crafts" into the search box to see examples.

You may also want to create subgroups on the Ning network that will give your customers more of a chance to talk about their jewelry interests. For example, if you have customers that wear jewelry for ceremonial purposes, then you can dedicate an entire forum to that subject. At the very least, this will make it easier for each person to join the group that interest them, as well as keep them focused on materials provided in more centralized locations.

The Ning software also gives you an ideal chance to learn more about your competitors. Invariably, you will find that other merchants will come to your site and look to market their products via signature lines, or creating soft sales pitches. Rather than trying to enforce "no solicitation" guidelines, you can charge these people a monthly fee to build a store on your network. Invariably, this will prevent the vast majority of people from using your network to compete with you.

On the other hand, individuals that are willing to pay a service fee can help you generate passive revenue with a minimal amount of difficulty.

DIGG

While most craft enthusiasts stop at Twitter, Facebook, LinkedIn or Ning, Digg is another site that must be explored. Digg is basically a social news site where visitors can promote content they find interesting. In 2008, Digg reported traffic of over 20 million visitors, so it's not a small site or a site to be trifled with. Having said that, there are a few things you should know before you begin to Digg.

To get your story to front page news is NOT easy. There's tough competition and a story is posted for 24 hours, during which time you really have to work to make sure it's "dugg" and votes are collected. Having said that, if you page does make it to front page, you can easily redirect over 10,000 unique visitors to your Etsy site through it.

How do you ensure a front-page story? By posting something sensational, breaking news, how-to guides or even interviews with known people. You'll need to be creative and come up with some ideas based on the kind of craft you do. Difficult, yes. Impossible, no.

Digging your own content obviously doesn't count, and doing so often may get you penalized. But you can research your community well and use the information to create content that will be popular (and dugg) and in this manner, market your store. You can also add videos to enhance your content or upload pictures and a story from your site or blog.

There are a few reasons you can use Digg, including:

- Adding friends
- "Digging" other craft sites
- Networking with other crafting enthusiasts

- Submitting your own work so others may Digg it

Signing on to Digg is fairly simple and once you've done that, begin by checking out the sites of friends or colleagues to see if they are on Digg. If they are, add them to your friends list. Now you have some people to starting Digging with.

In order to maximize the benefits of being on Digg, you do need to spend some time learning to use the resources at hand, and joining and understanding the communities on board. Digg is not for everyone, but if used correctly, can be an excellent means of driving traffic to your Etsy store.

Note: If the above link is broken, please visit www.digg.com and type "Arts and Crafts" into the search box.

STUMBLEUPON

Once you've been blogging for a while or have a well-designed Web site or store page to direct traffic to, you might want to consider using StumbleUpon. This is a social Web site that allows users to search for specific items (jewelry, felt bags, clay dolls, etc.) by clicking on a button on the StumbleUpon toolbar instead of a Google or Yahoo search. They're then randomly directed to Web sites that they can give a 'thumbs up' or 'thumbs down' to. StumbleUpon is a social bookmarking site that allows uses to bookmark their favorite sites and return to them, or share them with others.

- What does this mean for your Etsy store? Being on StumbleUpon will do the following:

- Make your site visible to a wider audience base

- Establish a regular base of potential customers via social bookmarking

- Cross link your site with others

Visit www.stumbleupon.com and type "Arts and Crafts" into the search box to see examples.

MUST HAVES ON ANY SOCIAL NETWORKING SITE

Before you sign up to any social media site, here are a few things to keep in mind to help you decide which ones are worth your time:

NETWORKING FEATURES

This is why you sign on, so do a bit of research to see if the features the site offers are suitable to your needs. Can you update your profile/page with photos of your latest creations? Can you send messages to more than one follower at a time? Make a list of your needs. Prioritize them and go through each social networking site you select to see how their features measure up.

A STRONG USER PROFILE

Your profile is what the world visits to learn more about you. Most sites will tell you to take extra care in crafting your profile and adding your picture of that of your craft. A user's profile should be fun, easy to understand, and speak volumes of your personality and your work.

SECURITY

You will be posting a lot of images and content, and perhaps negotiating sales through your social networking sites, so make sure the ones you sign up to have a strong security policy. Most of us skim through the 'user contract' without reading it. This is one instance where you should take the time to go through it and ensure the security on the site is strong.

SEARCH OPTIONS

Can you search within the site? More importantly, can your visitor search through your page to find what she needs? Most search options will allow you to conduct a search based on category, person or a product's name or key tag word.

ONLINE SUPPORT

If you are stuck, do you have regular access to a customer service representative? One of the biggest frustrations is trying to set up a site, facing some setbacks, and failing to find someone to address them. Does your social network provide you with adequate support?

You'll find most of the top social networking sites are well-regulated when it comes to both security and support, so if you are unfamiliar with the whole world of social networking, it's easier to sign to a more popular site like Twitter to get started. Once you find your footing, you can experiment with other sites.

THE RULES ABOUT NAVIGATING SOCIAL MEDIA SITES SUCCESSFULLY ARE SIMPLE

You will have to **sign up** for them, but doing so is easy, and they are all free. Make sure you fill out your bio and upload a nice picture of yourself or a selected piece of your craft. If your blog is set up, make sure you include your blog's URL and don't forget to add your Etsy store's URL.

Spend time on your selected sites to promote your store, but remember, it's easy to get distracted on these sites. You might have found an old crafting friend on Facebook and want to chat with her, or someone might have recommended links while on Twitter, which led you away from your project at hand. Establish a time frame – 30 minutes per day or one hour twice a week – and use it only for your promotions. Chatting and catching up can be done outside this timeframe.

Indulge in indirect promotion. An 80/20 rule works well, where 80 percent of the time you offer valuable advice and only 20 percent of the time you try and sell your Etsy store link. If you don't offer advice but only self-promote, you will be billed a "spammer" and can even get banned from certain sites.

Be yourself in all that you do. People who are passionate about engaging in social media are adept at spotting a fake. So stick to what you do, share your knowledge, and above all, be true to who you are. Those who eventually follow you and come to know you will be happy to shop at your store and support your endeavors.

Be consistent. When you first begin a group, fan page or discussion forum, you'll likely attend to it religiously for the first few weeks. But as time progresses, it often gets harder to keep up with maintaining this. If you find this is the case with your networking forays, it's best to re-evaluate your strategies immediately. Select one or two sites, depending on how much time per day/week you can devote to them, and stick to providing fresh content, updating messages, answering requests and participating in discussions on these sites. Don't bite off more than you can chew. If you find yourself getting a lot of business from your networking strategies, you might want to consider hiring someone – even a virtual assistant – to help you out on your sites. But that is worth it only if your can calculate how much business comes through networking. Until then, stick with what you can manage.

8 OTHER UNIQUE WAYS TO MARKET YOURSELF ONLINE

Marketing is an ongoing effort that is an investment of both time and effort and, in some cases, money. However, not all online marketing requires you to pay. You can see positive results simply by applying yourself to a few areas of marketing and focusing on them. Your marketing effort will make your Etsy shop visible, so devote some time each day toward making it work.

Once you've got your blog up and running, have signed on to a few networking sites, and have started building up your subscriber list, it's time to step it up a notch and branch out your marketing efforts to other areas. The following is a list of eight areas in which you can concentrate your marketing efforts. Doing so diligently will get you results!

1. Craft Web sites

There are hundreds of Web sites related to your topic that will be happy to showcase your work or your articles, for a fee, percentage of sales, or even a split of profits. Check out sites like Hand Made Spark (http://www.handmadespark.com/overview. php) as an example.

You will have to do your research to make sure the sites you contact are of a similar level to your site, are reputable, have a wide audience following and are compatible. Do a Google search using "(the site name) + scams" to see if any results crop up. You can also check for them on esty.com or the BBB (Better Business Bureau) to clear any doubts.

BEFORE APPROACHING THEM, HAVE A PLAN IN MIND:

- What is it you want to achieve?

- What is it you are willing to give them in return?

- How long would you like this working arrangement to last?

- Can you terminate this relationship if you don't see results?

- Likewise, can the Web site terminate the relationship and if so, how much notice do you get?

Next, you will want to see what form of advertising your offer can take – banners, logo exchanges and Web site links are all popular, and the latter can be a completely free way to exchange Web site information.

Always create a contract that has been prepared by a legal specialist to safeguard your rights, and if you are signing a contract prepared by the other Web site in question, have it read over by someone with legal knowledge.

Sites to check out include: http://etsymini. blogspot.com and We Love Etsy (http://etsylove. ning.com) And how do you promote yourself?

- Ask if you can do a banner exchange or a link exchange. The latter is good only if the site you are promoting yourself on has high traffic – otherwise, you might not draw much attention to your own site.

- You can also exchange guest posts on blogs. Your write on their blog and they write on yours. Don't forget to mention your store name and insert your Etsy link in your post.

- If you have a video, you can check to see if they will be open to sharing your video on their site.

- Likewise, you might also be able to do a showcase exchange, through which you showcase some of their crafts on your site, and they showcase some on yours on theirs. For this to work, the sites have to be complementary to each other, not direct competitors.

- Interviews on each other's blog or site might also work and they are similar to a guest post in that you can promote your Etsy store link quite well through them.

- And finally, check to see if the site has advertising options you can look into. While it might be more expensive to do this, if the site is a high-traffic zone with an audience similar to yours, it might be well worth the investment.

2. Ad Swaps

This works on a similar principle to Webvsite exchanges, and involves an equal exchange between two newsletters.

1. Have your Etsy store link added to their newsletter and in return, add their store link to your newsletter. As you will only be including a Web site name and link in both newsletters, this is a marketing method that can be repeated often.

2. Write a review of their store or include their products in an article in your newsletter and have them do the same for you. This approach can be stronger as it guarantees people will click on the link if the article is well written. However, you can use this method once or twice only as it involves an entire article being on display.

If you are not sure as to how to go about this, there are sites specifically designed to help you find an appropriate craft site you can exchange links with. They will select sites for you based on the number of subscribers and the compatibility of the site. Some sites to check out include AdSwap (www.adswap.com), ListSwapper (www.listswapper.com) and JV List Building (www.jvlistbuilding.com).

3. Telemarketing and Webinars

If you have something to market and are not doing so using a webinar, you might be losing out on sales. A webinar is a powerful tool that gives you the ability to sell to not tens, not even hundreds, but thousands of visitors online. This is more important if your craft can be explained online by a visual demonstration.

Why do videos work? Because they give you expert status. You share your honed techniques with your followers, who are keen to emulate you and create a similar craft. You know what to do, and now you share this information with others. Often marketing experts suggest you give the first webinar or video away for free and then begin to charge. Depending on how much promotion you've done in advance, you may even begin to share what you have with others for a package fee. This could include live demonstrations, video demonstrations, and even a printed guide.

Web conferences have another advantage to them. They help you build trust and gain a connection with your audience. Your audience gets to see you and know you better. And when the time comes to invite them back to your Etsy store to buy from you, they will be excited to do so.

Planning a Web conference or a video is easy. You just have to know where to begin. What will you be offering your audience? Is it a live demonstration? A series of uploaded videos? Will they be able to attend/download this for free? Paid for? Will it be like a lecture delivered? With humor? Will you get guest participants? (Like a YouTube demonstration, guest participants work very well on all video demonstrations, and if the guest is well known, you obviously will attract a larger audience to your show.)

If this is the first teleclass you'll be hosting, a good way to get a feel of how things are run is by joining one yourself and seeing firsthand how exciting it can be.

A note about uploading videos: You can create great videos using a Webcam, video camera or screen cast software. Once they are created, simply upload them on sites like TubeMogul and TrafficGeyser. The site www.slideshare.net also allows you to create professional PowerPoint presentations.

And once you've done this, don't forget to promote your class on the following free and paid for sites:

www.247coaching.com

www.planetteleclass.com

www.fullcalendar.com

www.cculearning.com

www.findfreeseminars.com

www.allconferences.com

You can also do a Google search to pull up listings of any seminars near you or that specialize in crafts.

And lastly, don't forget to track your results with a special tracking service such as on www. hypertracker.com.

4. Press Releases

Press releases are another great way to send out your news to hundreds of online readers and potential customers. They are an effective and often inexpensive way to get your message out. But again, as with any competitive field, you need to craft your message so it stands out from the rest. You can do so in the following way:

- **Write a strong headline**: Your headline is what will make your release stand out from the rest and draw attention to the content that follows, so spend some time writing a good and memorable one.

- **Short, tight copy**: Keep your copy short and on message. Ensure your message is included in the first paragraph, so editors and readers don't have to scroll down too far to get it.

- **Use quotes**: Quotes can be powerful if used correctly, so try and create some good ones, or use borrowed quotes, but be sure to gain permission before doing so.

- **Stick to the active tense**: The active voice is a stronger voice and carries your message further, so stick to it throughout the press release.

- **Add your contact information**: If you are including photographs of your work, be sure to mention you'll be adding them. Some online sites will charge you extra to print them. At the end of your press release, always include your name, your store's name, a contact detail and link to your site. A lot of online sites will not let you carry a link within your press release, but are happy to provide you with linking space in your contact information, so be sure to select your Etsy store's link for it.

Remember to optimize your press release with SEO content so that it gets picked up first by search engines and remains with higher rankings. *For more on how to optimize your content, please visit the earlier section: How to Optimize Web Content.*

Also keep the following in mind when it comes to optimizing your press release. Place keywords in the:

- **meta tag** (at the top bar of your browser)
- **meta descriptions and meta keywords**
- **press release title**
- **subtitle**
- **first paragraph**
- **end paragraph**

There are many further ways to draw attention to your Etsy site using press releases. The first point to remember is to **write press releases frequently**.

Using the above guidelines, you can create a press release each time you:

- **Create a batch of new craft items**
- **Diversify your line**
- **Develop a new take on an old problem**
- **Sponsor or participate in a craft event**
- **Launch a new craft-related program**
- **Provide expertise by way of videos, telecasts, etc.**

The next step is to distribute these press releases. You can find a lot of inexpensive and free online sites to distribute them through. Some of the top ones include:

1888PressRelease.com

24-7 Press Release

AddPR.com

BizEurope.com

eCommWire.com

Express-Press-Release.com

Free-Press-Release.com

Free-Press-Release-Center.info

FreePressIndex.com

FreePressRelease.co.cc

FreePressReleases.co.uk

i-Newswire.com

IndiaPRWire.com

PR.com

PR9.net

PR-Inside.com

PRlog.com

PRurgent.com

PRzoom.com

PressAbout.com

PressMethod.com

PressRelease.com

PressReleasePoint.com

TheOpenPress.com

And lastly, don't forget to **post your press release on your site** (under "media room") or blog. This will generate a further buzz and drive more traffic to your store.

5. Craigslist and Other Classified Ad Sites

From job hunters to homeowners wanting to get rid of unwanted furniture, everyone is posting on Craigslist. And you can't get a more cost-effective (it's free) method and wider audience than on this site. Founded in 1996, a mere 10 years later Craigslist was reported to have over 10 million unique visitors per day. You can place your ads by region or industry, which allows you to post to a targeted audience.

While you can sell anything on Craigslist, items like tutoring and retail ecommerce work really well. You can easily promote your Etsy store link or your newsletter. Everyone loves a giveaway and you will have people signing up for your newsletter if they think they can get value from it. Similarly, the promise of a free gift or a discount coupon might also have them clicking on your Etsy store link or visiting your Web site or blog.

Firstly, start by **identifying your target market**. In which city or cities are you going to post your ad? Posting an ad – nationally or locally – requires you to follow a set of rules. For example, you can't over-post your ad and you definitely can't spam or use Craigslist to build your mailing list. Doing so can get you banned from using the site. Before your begin, write out the ad you want to place. Remember you should not post the same ad within 48 hours of first uploading it, so create new ads depending on what you want to say. Not only does Craigslist keep tabs on who is spamming, users can also 'flag' an ad, so be careful with your wording.

You can upload images to your ad, so select the ones you want to use (a homemade candle, or a piece of jewelry, or a pot of homemade lip salve), choosing an image that is striking in design and color. Search results are based on date they first appear, and only then by keyword. You should still incorporate your keywords so they get picked up. An ad with an image on is proven to be more effective, so don't hesitate to select one or more images.

Get straight to the point. Most Craigslist users are leery of ads that sound spammy or don't provide enough information, so be specific and include a name and link back so it is more authentic.

While Craigslist does not provide a built-in tracking mechanism, you can use your Web site's link, email address or phone number to **track the effectiveness** of the ad. The easiest way to do this is to create a separate Yahoo or Gmail email address and use it only for your Craigslist responses.

Both buyers and sellers on Craigslist are **susceptible to fraud** simply because of the anonymity it provides. Just as buyers might be hesitant to buy directly from the site, the seller must also be cautious. Use Craigslist to redirect interested buyers to your Etsy link rather than to try and sell directly on Craigslist. If you do want to sell directly, ensure you take precautionary measures, such as talking to the customer on the phone, shipping out only once full payment is received, and asking for an address and contact details you can verify.

6. Joint Promotion With Other Etsy Store Owners

Joint promotions can work really well when carried out in conjunction with stores that complement your products, not compete with them. Therefore, if you sell handmade paper, you might be able to work closely with a card-creating venture, or if you sell handmade face creams, you can tie up with a handmade cosmetics company. The options are endless if you do a bit of research and careful planning.

When considering a joint venture with a fellow artist, keep in mind the following courtesies:

It's important to give before you receive. Sure, you might be in it for the fame and money, but a joint venture also needs to be respectful and appreciative of each other's successes before it can become a long-term partnership. Don't ask for too much and remember that each business is there to try and promote itself as best it can. Similarly, try and see how you best complement each other's business. Often putting two heads together can lead to some tremendously successful ideas.

You don't have to feel passionate about the other person's product, but you still have to like it. Only then will you feel comfortable tying with them. The same goes for the other party's personality. It has to complement yours.

Keep your business head on. While you might be friends with the person you will be tying up with, remember that in the end it's a business deal and your accounts and individual job descriptions should be in order no matter what kind of joint promotion you enter into.

7. Voice Mails

While most of us think of voice mail as a boring message to let you know the owner of a store or resident of a home is unavailable, voice mail can actually be effective as a marketing tool. You basically have three phone options: your home phone, your store phone, and your cell phone. You can harness all three to create effective messages directing people to your Etsy site. You can also offer them the chance to sign up for your newsletter.

If you use an online service like www.skype.com, check to see if you can update your voice mail on it. Have a sale? Leave a voice message to that effect. Offering an instant discount to purchases of over $50? Change your message to announce it. The best part about voice messages is that they can be changed as often as you like. Just remember to include your Etsy link or newsletter offer on them.

8. Thank-You Emails and Notes

Saying "thank you" to a buyer or someone who inquires about a product is not only considered good form, it can also convert into more sales for you. If you mail out your products, consider putting in a brief thank-you note with a link to your site. You can also ask for referrals or include additional business cards with a note requesting they be forwarded to friends. This is an excellent way of marketing your store while at the same time getting to know customers a little better. You can also ask your customer if he would like to sign up to receive your emails and use this method to build up your database.

If you don't want to send out a note, a simple thank-you email works well and allows you to include a bit about your Etsy store and its link. You can also offer an incentive to get visitors to make further purchases, like a discount coupon for their next purchase or a "buy one, get one free" deal the next time they visit your store.

CHAPTER EIGHT

Promoting Your Jewelry Offline

W hen you work with online marketing, there is always a tendency to ignore the fact that a great deal of commerce still goes on away from the Internet. Without a question, when you are looking for new customers, part of your job will include drawing people to your Web-based store. Therefore, if you want to be successful as a home-based jewelry designer, you will need to spend a good bit of time developing a business presence right in your own community.

THE BENEFITS OF PROMOTING YOUR JEWELRY OFFLINE

Marketers that work in an online environment often have a difficult time determining what aspects of their sales pitch needs adjusting. On the other hand, when you speak with someone face to face or on the phone, you can learn more from their body language and tone of voice. This will give you a number of opportunities to gauge how well your sales pitches will work in other environments.

Consider a situation where you are trying to develop slogans to use on your Web site and in your advertisements. While you may think that a particular comment is amusing, someone else may be offended by it. Chances are, if you ask enough people, you will get a good idea about what the average person thinks about your slogans. Once you try these marketing plans out on a small audience, you will reduce the risk of causing damage to your online presence.

Even though you may be in the very early stages of developing your business, you will always need to think about the future. A slogan that looks fresh and exciting today may look boring and hackneyed in a matter of weeks. This, in turn, means that you are always going to need the opinions of other people in order to help you gauge new sales pitches.

As may be expected, when you market your jewelry offline, you will also have a chance to make more sales. In fact, if other people in your local area are busy trying to sell their wares online, you may be able to enjoy a slightly reduced level of competition at the local level. These individuals can be leveraged to help you gain testimonials for your site.

In many cultures, there is a tendency for people to want to know what your neighbors or friends think of you. Even though you may form friendships and business dealings with thousands of people online, some people still wonder how you behave in your own community. When you fail to provide that information, it can be very difficult for people to gain a sense of your character. This, in turn, makes it a bit harder for them to empathize with you. As may be expected, when you are trying to appeal to someone's emotions, there is nothing worse than appearing like a brick wall or a stranger. While your customers may never contact people in your local community, knowing that you have this type of support in your life still creates a positive and meaningful impression.

SOME IMPORTANT TOOLS

When you promote your jewelry offline, potential consumers will not have a chance to bookmark your site and view it at a later date. Unfortunately, if they do not remember the name of your business, they will have a very hard time finding you again. This is just one of many reasons why you should always have some type of literature on hand to give to consumers. Among other things, you should have a business card that features your logo and store URL. You may also want to create flyers and pamphlets that can be given away for free.

If you are going to work with business cards and flyers, you may wind up distributing thousands of sales pieces in a short period of time. In some cases, you may be able to purchase pre-fabricated items from a professional printing service. On the other hand, if you want the maximum amount of flexibility, then you will be well served by purchasing a good quality printer, paper supplies, and an image-editing program. At the very least, if you find that one of your sales pitches does not work out very well, you won't have to worry about having wasted money on professional services.

Individuals that plan to market jewelry offline usually need to have a good bit of confidence. As you go from one location to another, you may get a lot of rejections. Rather than take these matters personally, you will need to keep going until you succeed. No matter how much you may want to give up, you never really know when you will find someone that will be amenable to your plans. Once you find that person, you may just reach dozens of other people that will be interested in buying your jewelry.

In a sense, you can think about places where you can leave your store literature as tools. While you may be tempted to only approach merchants, there are many other businesses that deal with the general public. This includes medical, accounting, and lawyer offices, as well as community service agencies and colleges. As may be expected, you will need to gain permission to leave your literature in a prominent place. Depending on the situation, you may want to bring along a few free samples of your jewelry as gifts.

JEWELRY PLACEMENT IN LOCAL STORES

Oddly enough, many entrepreneurs believe that they have to rent their own store, or try to build a store on their own. Nevertheless, if you go to a local department store, everything on the shelves is actually created by manufacturers that do not own the store. Typically, the store owner will charge the manufacturer a commission in exchange for displaying the items. In addition, the store also charges the customer a higher price for the item.

When you first start selling jewelry, you may not be able to afford to sell your items in the larger department stores. On the other hand, if there are small boutiques nearby, you may be able to gain shelf space at a reasonable price. This will also be an ideal time to bring along business cards that can be given to patrons of the boutique.

Even if a handful of people decide to look up your Web site, it will be to your advantage. At the very least, if they do not purchase anything from you, they may still forward your link to friends that may be interested in your jewelry.

If you are having a hard time finding store owners to work with, you should join your local chamber of commerce. As you attend various meetings, you will gain plenty of insight into business operations, as well as the concerns of other business owners. In addition, you may just meet store owners that you had not considered approaching. For example, if you meet someone that owns a supermarket, you may learn that he/she needs novel items to promote some type of event. Even if your jewelry is only displayed for a week or two in conjunction with your business card, it will serve as a key opportunity to increase the visibility of your business.

CRAFT FAIRS AND TRADE SHOWS

There is no question that craft fairs generate an enormous amount of excitement in a local community. If you can rent a booth at one of these events, you should be prepared to sell a good bit of jewelry. As may be expected, gauging the number of items to bring along may be a bit difficult.

Ideally you should bring along items to sell, as well as items that remain on the table for display. If you run out of certain pieces, then you can always provide a business card that lists your Web site. This may also be an ideal time to obtain the customer's name and ask if he/she wants to place the item on backorder. Even though your potential customer may be disappointed at not being able to make a purchase on the spot, he/she can still look forward to obtaining the jewelry at a later date. Needless to say, you should fill these orders as quickly as possible.

Craft fairs and trade shows also provide an ideal opportunity to gain more information from customers. This includes opinions about fashion trends and community events. When other people are willing to discuss life events and experiences with you, then you will also have something to work with as you create new signature pieces.

When you work with people at a craft fair, they may tell you about things going on in their family, as well as items in the news that made an impression on them. If you find something that has a strong emotional resonance, then you may be able to take that sentiment and fashion it into some type of jewelry. For example, if someone is grieving over someone that passed on from cancer, you may want to create a bracelet or other item that can be worn by people that share the same experience.

While you are at a trade show, you should never overlook the opportunity to see what other jewelry designers are developing. In some cases, this may make it a bit easier for you to define your own style. Among other things, if you were thinking to use gold charms on bracelets, you may see dozens of other designers working with the same idea. If you feel that the market is saturated with these items, then you might choose to work with silver charms, or even plastic ones that feature different colors.

CREATING YOUR OWN COMMUNITY EVENT

Depending on the size of your community, you may find that there are very few craft fairs to attend. Why not create community events on your own? For example, you may want to host a summer picnic, or even have a yard sale every weekend. No matter which venue you choose, you will always need to look for ways to sell jewelry to visitors, as well as provide information about your online store.

If you are going to create a community event, it is important to make sure that you do not need special permits or permission from the town board. In most cases, a simple call to the town clerk will guide you in the right direction. For example, in some locales, you may not need to have a permit, but you may have to observe a curfew. This is especially important to consider if you want to start a community event in a city, or some other area where there are concerns about public safety and the potential for blocking roadways.

CHARITY WORK AND FUNDRAISERS

For some strange reason, people always assume that business owners have more money than anyone else. Regardless of whether it comes to tax brackets, utility costs, or dealing with others in your community, people will always expect you to spend more than an average consumer. Unfortunately, the vast majority of business owners do not have much money, especially when they are just starting out.

Many business owners today look to raise money for charities or attend fundraisers in order to increase the visibility of their business. If you visit local churches, you can probably learn about all kinds of causes that benefit local community members. Chances are, if you attend these events on a regular basis and offer your jewelry, you can draw a good bit of attention to your products. Depending on the venue, you may also be able to keep at least some of the money that comes in.

When you work with charity events and fundraisers, you will also have a chance to meet some very influential people in your community. They may include doctors, lawyers and other people that advocate for various causes. As these people return to their regular occupations, they may also carry information about your jewelry with them. Therefore, you should always be prepared to offer stacks of business cards or flyers that lead back to your Web site. If these individuals are interested in raising money for special causes, they may also be willing to purchases a larger quantity of jewelry from you.

Depending on your outlook, you may find that the interests of people in your local community do not always match yours. For example, while many people may be interested in raising money to help take care of stray cats and dogs, few may be interested in raising money to protect and take care of penguins. Rather than create an unsuccessful venue in your local community, you may want to locate your event to another geographic region.

If you are looking for people that share common interests, you are bound to find plenty of sites online. As you meet people from different communities, you can create a map that will reveal where heavy concentrations of like-minded people live. Once you have this information in hand, then you can begin making plans to host your venue in that neighborhood.

Even though you will need to coordinate a number of things from a distance, at least you will have satisfaction knowing that the event will be successful. This will also be an ideal time to see how people from other parts of the country view your products. No doubt, once you return home from the event in question, you will be filled with all kinds of inspiration that can be turned into new and exciting signature jewelry pieces.

WORKING WITH THE LOCAL MEDIA

There is no question that having your business showcased on the local news can be of immense benefit. Individuals that are organizing a fundraiser, or some other type of community event, may want to contact radio and TV stations. If these stations also support streaming content online, then you may also be able to ask them to showcase your business online. Needless to say, when you can gain online and offline coverage, it will be of immense benefit.

Chances are, if you watch the local news, you will always take note of the jewelry worn by the news anchors. As you may be aware, wardrobe information is usually presented in the closing credits of most television shows. Therefore, if you give news anchors free jewelry, it may be a useful way to gain some publicity for your products. While they may not always post a link to your Web site in the closing credits, people that search for your business name should be able to find you. Check all the major search engines to make sure that this information is easy to find.

There is nothing quite like a broken computer, loss of Internet capability, or a power outage to send you scrambling for a phonebook. Even if you have not looked in the yellow pages for years on end, other people rely on them in order to find businesses. In many cases, even if you only apply for a free link in the yellow pages, it may be well worth your while.

Needless to say, if you are interested in online classified ads, you may also want o advertise in your local newspapers. This method of advertising can easily be combined with fundraisers, as well as other venues that will enhance your business image. In some cases, you may also be able to get a free listing for the name of your business if you become part of featured community events.

INTERVIEW WITH ETSY ENTHUSIAST
GLASS DESIGNER ROBERT JOYNER

When did you start your business and what motivated you to work with glass?

I am a carpenter by trade and have always worked with my hands to create unique pieces. With the downturn in the economy and the decline in work here in Ireland, I began looking at alternative ways to earn money. I knew my passion lay in working with my hands, so I began looking for ways to use my skills. I had read about glass fusion before and this is the area I returned to look at. I began reading up about it and found a course in Ireland that I could do.

I couldn't believe how naturally it came to me and how much I enjoy the designing process. I purchased all the equipment necessary and began creating pieces in my workshop at home. I knew that I would also be able to incorporate my woodworking skills into the glass-fusing process and this was an added bonus.

You already have your Web site, so what made you think of setting up shop on Etsy?

I had my Web site set up but wasn't well up on the marketing side of things. My wife knows more about this and is taking over for me. I started looking online to see where I could sell my pieces and that is when I found Etsy. I decided to give this Web site a trial run to see if it was something that I could use in my marketing efforts.

I set up an account and placed two items on the Web site; a fused-glass clock and one of my fused-glass pendants. There was also a link back to my own Web site.

You don't use traditional marketing methods on Etsy such as showcasing your work. Why is that?

To be completely honest, I haven't used all the options available to crafters on Etsy because I haven't needed to. With the initial two products that I put on display I had a massive boost in traffic to my own Web site. The fused-glass clock that I had on display got a lot of attention and this led to a lot of inquiries via my own Web site.

I found that in my first trial month on Etsy my Web site traffic increased by over 300 percent, which was benefit enough for me. I have an online store, so selling my products on Etsy wasn't my main objective. My main objective was to get my name out there and my Web site known, which I really did achieve.

What has your response been so far on the site?

The response that I have received from Etsy has been amazing. It cost me just $.04 per month per item and the sales and contacts I have made have been phenomenal. I have been contacted by people all over the world in relation to my fused-glass clocks and it has really helped to establish me as a fused-glass artist.

My sales have received a significant boost and when I check my Google analytics to see where the traffic is coming from I am finding it is from Etsy. I have also had people contact me who saw my pieces on Etsy wondering if I could create custom pieces for them. I have designed five different fused-glass clocks for wedding presents so far and I have orders for another four. It really has made such a huge difference to my marketing and I am delighted to have found it.

Are there any other marketing techniques you would recommend to Etsy users?

My wife has taken over the marketing aspect of things for me. She is currently working on a new Web site that will include a blog for search engine optimization purposes and to help with organic traffic. She has also advised me to submit my Web site to the various crafts directories and I have also signed up with a couple of excellent crafts forums where I can chat with like-minded people, answer questions, and of course, promote my own Web site and work. She also created a Twitter account so that I can let everyone know about new pieces and she is working on a Facebook fan page. She has been teaching me about social networking and bookmarking to make the most of the marketing side of things.

I think all Etsy users should make sure that they have their own Web sites where potential customers can contact them. This has worked out amazingly well for me and I have had a lot of people contact me. People want to know about the different pieces that I can make and if there is somewhere that they can view them in person.

If there was one piece of marketing advice you could offer, what would it be?

Learn about social networking. It is a great way to get people to notice your work and a great way to bring in new customers.

Is there anything else you'd like to add about Jace Glass Designs?

Jace Glass Designs creates unique pieces of fused-glass art and jewelry. All pieces are handmade and different from each other. I don't use molds for my fused-glass pendants, which makes them totally unique. I also work on creating custom pieces and personalized pieces, such as anniversary and birthday plates.

CONCLUSION

No matter how talented you may be, there will come a time when you need to start sharing your products with other people. If you want to be a successful businessperson, then you will constantly need to be concerned with finding and managing customers. Even though that may seem like a daunting process, there are many tools available to help you.

Not so long ago, some of the most successful merchants on Etsy.com were in your position. They knew they had a talent for designing jewelry, but they did not know how to go about making a living from that ability. Many of these people went through a process of trial and error when it came to various aspects of their business. Unfortunately, for every person that succeeds, there are dozens that fail. Still, others go on blundering for years on end without seeming to make headway.

Rather than try to blunder along, you can use the advice offered in this book in order to avoid some of the most common pitfalls. At the same time, you can also think about each aspect of your business, and make sure that these elements move you toward success instead of failure. In some cases, something as simple as knowing how to set your prices can mean the difference between bankruptcy and making more money than you ever dreamed possible. You are also bound to find that having a guidebook will give you a bit of inspiration for taking each step.

If you happen to go for a walk in the woods during the springtime, you may notice all kinds of seeds on the ground. No matter whether they are – pine cones or maple seeds – each one of them has the potential to grow into an enormous tree that will benefit the forest and all its inhabitants. In a similar way, your new business also has the potential to play a powerful role in the world. Regardless of whether you dedicate your jewelry-making efforts toward charity events, or simply uplifting people's moods, you will always be able to enjoy knowing that you are contributing to an amazing adventure.

We hope that you enjoyed this book, and that you are filled with motivation to start making plans for your new store at Etsy.com. Without a doubt, once you see your business starting to grow, you will realize why so many other people have decided to embrace the challenges of this type of career. In fact, when you look back on your first tentative steps toward owning your own jewelry business, you are likely to smile and be very glad that you made the jump, as this is a career choice that will allow you to fulfill your passion, work daily on something that you love and earn a living being creative and independent. That's a recipe for success – now that you've got all of the right tools and information to help you get started!

Good luck!

CPSIA information can be obtained at www.ICGtesting.com
Printed in the USA
LVOW10*1510130415

434396LV00006B/110/P